ONCE AROUND THE SUN

FROM CAMBODIA TO TIBET

JESSICA MUDDITT

HEMBURY
—BOOKS—

Once Around the Sun - From Cambodia to Tibet

By Jessica Mudditt

© 2024

www.jessicamudditt.com.au

Hembury Books

All rights reserved. No portion of this book may be reproduced in any form without permission from the publisher, except as permitted by Australian copyright law.

Cover photo taken in Yangshuo, China by Blick Winkel/Alamy

CONTENTS

About the Author   v
Dedication   vii
Prologue   ix

1. Chasing the sun   1
2. More than I could chew   7
3. Dark red rouge   16
4. Mr Bellisimo   22
5. The lost kingdom   33
6. Have backpack, will teach   44
7. Island life   59
8. Lost and found   68
9. The banana pancake trail   76
10. Hanoi hustle   89
11. Bad backpackers   102
12. Ding dong   111
13. The man   135
14. Lonely planet   142
15. My good fortune   150
16. Rags to riches   163
17. Bright lights, big city   175
18. Friendships in the Qing dynasty   190
19. Double happiness   205
20. In or out?   217
21. Trouble in paradise   229
22. Sky high   251

Thanks for reading   265

ABOUT THE AUTHOR

Jessica Mudditt is the author of *Our Home in Myanmar – Four Years in Yangon*. This first memoir describes the period she worked as a journalist in Myanmar.

Once Around the Sun is a two-part memoir describing her year-long backpacking journey in 2006, which took place six years before she moved to Myanmar. The second instalment is called *Kathmandu to the Khyber Pass* and it will be published in 2025.

Jessica is also the founder of Hembury Books, which provides coaching, editing and self-publishing services to nonfiction authors. She founded the business in 2023 to help other indie authors navigate the self-publishing journey.

During her 15-year career as a journalist, Jessica's articles were published by Forbes, BBC, CNN, and the Economist Intelligence Unit. She spent ten years working in London, Myanmar and Bangladesh before returning to Australia in 2016. She currently lives in Sydney with her two daughters and two cats.

For anyone who has ever wanted to go anywhere or be anything.

PROLOGUE

For a long time I believed that the year I spent backpacking through Asia didn't warrant a book. First of all, it was too common an experience. Most people I knew had gone backpacking in their twenties, although perhaps not for quite as long as I did. I assumed the reason I'd never come across a book describing a backpacker's travels was because there was too much fun and hedonism involved. Aren't memoirs supposed to be about the toughest stuff we face in life?

Then the COVID-19 pandemic struck in early 2020, and international travel went out the window. I felt so sorry for the young people who had to cancel their backpacking plans. I read media reports suggesting that travellers may never return to India, or at least not to certain parts that were seeing a shockingly high number of COVID-19 deaths. It was suggested that health precautions and social distancing restrictions could remain in place there indefinitely.

Soon after the lockdowns began, I saw a cartoon on Facebook that got me thinking. In it a bookshop owner quipped to a customer, 'We've moved our travel books into the fantasy section.' I began to see my overland journey from Cambodia to

Pakistan in a different light. If young people never got to travel with the same absolute freedom that I experienced, I wanted to at least document how magical it had been.

By the time I'd finished mapping out the chapters of this book, I'd realised that while backpacking is indeed one of life's greatest pleasures, it can also be confronting, challenging and uncomfortable. And profoundly lonely. When I travelled in 2006, I had never even heard of social media. I stayed in touch with friends and family by checking my emails at an internet café every few days. Outside of those visits, I was on my own. I carried a basic Nokia mobile phone, but I only used it as an alarm clock. Sometimes the loneliness was overwhelming, but I'm grateful to have experienced being far from home and truly disconnected.

My year of backpacking gave me self-confidence. Even now, nearly twenty years later, when I have to do something that makes me nervous I remember how I travelled to far-flung places on my own. I draw strength from that and tell myself that I can therefore do whatever it is I have to do.

Travelling opened my eyes to poverty and inequality, and it made me realise I wanted to become a journalist. It also marked the start of a fascination with Asia, where I returned to live for another seven years. My first book, *Our Home in Myanmar*, describes the four years I lived in Myanmar from 2012 to 2016. I will also write a memoir about the three years I spent in Bangladesh.

Initially, I wasn't sure if I could remember my trip well enough to provide the detail needed for a book. I'd written long diary entries while I was away, but those diaries had been lost in London. What made this book possible is the fact that my wonderful dad meticulously saved every email I sent him. When I returned home after what ended up being a decade overseas, Dad handed me the storage drive containing all our emails from my big backpacking adventure. Another few years passed before I opened the drive, and I was stunned to discover that our emails came to 86,000 words – about the length of a book.

Sadly, my dad passed away before I'd finished writing this memoir, so he will never get to read it. My adventurous spirit caused him a lot of worry, and I would have loved for him to have seen me produce something from my travels that could be enjoyed from the safety of an armchair.

Of course, my mum also worried. Now I'm a mother, I understand how parents must feel when their children leave home for a trip on a shoestring budget. But, possibly despite her better judgement, Mum supported me anyway. It was Mum who saved the long letters I wrote to my grandmother every month, and every postcard I ever sent home. I joke that she is my book agent because she's always looking out for opportunities for me.

I also got back in touch with many of the people I met on my travels, and asked if my memories stacked up against theirs. My thanks go to Romi, Paula, Les, Josiah, Clem, Bruce and Phil for their help.

The process of reconstructing past events also involved combing through my photos and watching endless YouTube videos made by other travellers of the places I'd been. I've spent many hours taking online walking tours, and I also bought the 2006 editions of Lonely Planet guidebooks from second-hand booksellers to find the places I stayed and sights I visited. Happily, memories of the most formative year of my life came flooding back. I could even sometimes picture the internet café where I sent a particular email from.

As I wrote and wrote and the word length grew, I realised I was writing not one book, but two. *Once Around the Sun: From Cambodia to Tibet* describes the first six months of my year-long journey. *Kathmandu to the Khyber Pass* will describe the second half, which covers my time in Nepal, India and Pakistan.

During the interminably long COVID-19 lockdowns in Sydney and in between caring for two very young children as a single parent, it has been a tonic to relive the freest year of my life. I hope that you share my joy in recounting the experience, and that it encourages others to explore our beautiful planet.

1
CHASING THE SUN

Phnom Penh's dusty streets were filled with a cacophony of honking horns, rumbling motorcycle engines, generators and jackhammers. Tuktuks and motorbikes far outnumbered the cars on the road, and the footpath was crammed with all manner of things being sold, parked or repaired. The traffic moved slowly yet fluidly, with green and red lights routinely ignored. When my taxi rattled to a stop behind a bank-up of cars, a motorbike rider simply mounted the kerb and went around us.

It wasn't until we took a right at a roundabout that I realised we were driving on the opposite side of the road from what I was used to in Australia. For the first ten minutes of the journey from the airport, I had been too busy gaping like a goldfish at the parallel universe I seemed to have landed in.

The taxi pulled up out the front of my first home away from home: Tat Guesthouse, in the city's central south. It was a three-storey apartment with shuttered garage doors and a tiered roof in need of a lick of paint. I entered a dark passage crammed with bicycles and the pleasant smell of incense.

'Welcome to the kingdom of Cambodia,' said a young guy on

reception when I told him I'd made a reservation from Australia. He grinned then stubbed out a cigarette and grabbed a key from the hook behind him, motioning for me to follow him up a flight of stairs.

'The showers and bathroom are here,' he said, pointing to a couple of Perspex doors as we made our way along a narrow corridor. 'The rooftop restaurant is up those stairs. You'll meet other travellers there and we have some computers for sending emails.'

He stopped at a door further down the corridor, unlocked it and gently pushed it open.

'This is your room,' he said. 'You need to pay for each night in advance, before noon.'

As I stepped past him, I did a double take: my room looked like a prison cell. In the shadows was a single bed that took up virtually all the floor space. I felt for a light switch. A naked fluorescent bulb halfway up the wall flickered noisily for several seconds, seemingly reluctant to be used. I took a couple of steps and pulled back the flimsy curtain, revealing a view of another apartment block so close that I could have reached out and touched it, had bars not been installed across the window. The paint on the walls was peeling and a trail of ants ran across at eye level. I turned around to the young man, but he had already disappeared down the hall.

Don't panic. This is fine.

I unfastened the straps of my backpack and placed it on the ground, but then I had to step over it to get onto the bed. The mattress creaked and sagged beneath my weight. I sighed and reached over to turn on the pedestal fan, which made an almighty clacking sound. Boy was it hot.

So this was what a two-dollar room looked like. In deciding where to stay in Phnom Penh, I had combed my *Cambodia Lonely Planet* for the cheapest room at the cheapest guesthouse.

After I got a reply from Tat Guesthouse confirming my booking, I'd congratulated myself for being so thrifty. I was having some serious regrets now.

Staying in the two-dollar room was a depressing prospect, but I knew I'd feel guilty if I swapped it for a more expensive one. It would be pretty typical of me though; money seemed to slip through my fingers like sand. I desperately wanted to be good at budgeting while I was away, because it had taken me over a year to save up enough money for my big trip.

I couldn't decide what to do and it was too hot to sleep, even though I was tired from the overnight flight. I went to the shared bathroom and splashed cold water on my face. Then I headed up to the breezy rooftop area. Over a pineapple juice and a plate of fried rice, I met a couple from New Zealand called Phil and Deb. They had arrived in Cambodia a few days earlier after island hopping through Thailand, which I'd done a few years ago after a brief sojourn through Western Europe. I immediately clicked with Phil and Deb – when I told them that I had no intention of pursuing a career in law despite having obtained a degree in it, I didn't need to explain myself any further. Back home, I was usually asked what I would be doing instead of law (often with the inference that there was nothing better). When I conceded that I didn't know – I just knew that law was not for me – I'd be met with raised eyebrows or even clucks of disapproval. I'm sure many people thought I was a bit of a loser. Career-wise, I was the black sheep in a family of three daughters. My eldest sister Alice was passionate about her work in occupational therapy, and my other sister Nancy had obtained a law degree and was actually a practicing lawyer.

Phil and Deb happily told me how had both quit their jobs to travel for eight months. They saw work as a means of being able to travel, which I found refreshing. We said how excited we were to be in Cambodia and agreed that travel was the elixir of life.

While swapping travel notes, Deb told me they were staying in a five-dollar room, and that she was amazed by what good value Cambodia was. I replied that my 'prison cell' room was depressing, but that I felt I should stay in it regardless.

'We can afford the more expensive room because we're a couple,' said Deb sympathetically. 'For us it's only two dollars fifty each.'

'That's true,' I said. 'I need to be careful not to spend too much on accommodation or it'll blow out my budget.'

'Or maybe set yourself a rule that you only drink beers every second day and save money that way?' suggested Phil helpfully.

'I'd like to see you try that, Phil,' Deb said with a grin.

But despite the higher costs that came with being a solo traveller, I was happy to be on my own. I was free to decide where I went and what I saw without needing to accommodate anyone else's preferences. When my boyfriend had dumped me a few months back, I'd told myself over and over that it was actually a good thing, because now I was free to enjoy what I had nicknamed my 'Chase the Sun Tour'. I had left Melbourne on 1 June 2006, the first day of winter, and after spending exactly three hundred sixty-five days in the tropics, I would arrive in London on 1 June 2007, the first day of the British summer.

I followed one of Phil and Deb's sightseeing tips by heading to the national museum in a cyclo, a three-wheeled cycle-rickshaw where the passenger sits in a carriage in front of the driver. I leaned back into the comfortable bucket seat and gazed idly at the jumble of shopfronts, above which hung Khmer-language billboards and thick reams of powerlines. Women and children were going about their day in colourful patterned pyjamas – was it some kind of fashion trend? I counted a family of five on a motorbike, including a baby wedged between his mother and father. But the sight that really took my breath away that afternoon was a monk on a scooter. He was sitting side-saddle behind a driver, his bright-orange robes blowing in the hot breeze and a serene half-smile on his face. On his lap was – of all things – a computer monitor. I felt about a million miles away from Melbourne, and I couldn't stop grinning. Even so, I felt bad for the thin old man behind me dripping sweat as he pumped the pedals to get me to my destination.

I was so weary that I was unable to absorb much about the Khmer artefacts inside the museum. After about an hour I headed out to the street-food stalls that I'd noticed on my way in. A woman in a floral apron was manning an enormous wok on wheels. It was filled with noodles covered in a soy glaze. Beside it was a glass cabinet containing shredded carrot, bean sprouts and spring onions. I nodded at the woman, and she cracked an egg into the wok, and then scooped out enough noodles to fill a polystyrene container as it cooked. She asked me for 1000 riels, the equivalent of thirty American cents. Thirty cents! Suddenly craving a caffeine hit, I asked her for a Coca-Cola, and handed over another three hundred riels. To my surprise, she opened the can and tipped its contents into a small plastic bag. I stared at her incredulously. Saying nothing, she popped a straw into the bag and passed it over to me with a smile. I took a seat on a plastic stool and dug in. The noodles were delicious, and drinking Coke out of a bag was fun, although I had to finish it in one go or else spill it everywhere. As I downed the last dregs, I realised that I was being eyed off by a little street kid with a grubby face and matted hair. Behind him stood a man in rags with only one leg; I assumed he was the boy's father. I felt bad, so I shouted them a serving of noodles.

I was jubilant to discover that street food was even cheaper than I'd imagined. If I stuck with eating only this, I could offset the cost of a more expensive room. Brilliant!

When I returned to my guesthouse, I asked the young man if he could show me a five-dollar room. Just as Phil and Deb had said, it was enormous by comparison, with two double beds and a TV, plus my own shower and toilet.

'I'll take it,' I said, beaming.

I gleefully set out my toiletries in the bathroom. It's good to have a bit of nous, I thought.

Despite being exhausted from my long-haul journey, I made the most of having a television and watched a bizarre Chinese game show I couldn't make head nor tail of. I relished how alien it seemed: it was yet more proof that I had swapped my life of dull familiarity and aimlessness for something a whole lot better. I drifted into unconsciousness, blissful in the knowledge that a year of discovery and adventure lay ahead.

2

MORE THAN I COULD CHEW

I spent the next few days developing a new rhythm to my life as a traveller. I was overjoyed that I no longer needed to set the alarm to be up and ready early for another dull day of administrative duties at the publishing company I had been working at. For an entire year, I could sleep until I naturally woke up.

When I woke around nine, I showered and took my malaria pill, then headed straight out for something to eat. For breakfast, I usually had a toasted French baguette with chicken, pâté, salad and spring onions, which I bought from a man with a missing front tooth who ran a snack cart on the street corner near Tat Guesthouse. I washed it down with a coffee from one of the plentiful cafes. Baguettes and excellent coffee were the culinary legacy of almost a century of French colonial rule. In Cambodia, however, a white coffee wasn't the kind I was used to. Sweetened condensed milk was substituted for cow's milk; I assumed because it wouldn't sour in the sun if refrigeration were an issue during power cuts. I'd started taking my coffee black to avoid the sugar hit.

With a full belly and loaded up on caffeine, I would then

happily set off to explore Cambodia's capital, which inevitably involved walking several kilometres. To my delight I was realising that it was me who set the pace. Whether it be a tourist site or a city, I would linger for as long as it held my interest, and then I was free to move on. My daily life was so wondrous that I almost couldn't believe it was real. I oohed and aahed over the golden Royal Palace, sweated my way through the souvenir stalls at the Russian Market, took a sunset cruise along the silty Mekong River and swatted away a creepy old man at a pagoda on a hilltop, who first demanded a tip and then tried to grab my boob.

I also met a few other backpackers at Tat Guesthouse, and I hadn't come across anyone who wasn't up for a chat. I was excited to be meeting people from all corners of the globe, and it meant that my ex-boyfriend Matthew was definitely taking a backseat in my thoughts, which I was pleased about. From time to time I impulsively wondered what he would think of something I saw, or if I would rise in his estimation if he knew that I had seen it.

It had been a little over two months since I had been in touch with Matthew. I had been too embarrassed to contact him after the 'Night of Disaster', which was when I made a complete fool of myself. And yet I hadn't given up all hope of redeeming myself. Against my better judgement I told myself that a few witty travel anecdotes from overseas provided my best chance. I may even get a reply from him.

On one of these early days in the city, after buying a set of loose-fitting pyjamas to sleep in and a pair of cotton fisherman pants that I had seen other backpackers wearing, I stopped in for an afternoon beer at the hallowed Foreign Correspondents' Club. I climbed the stairs of the pastel-yellow, colonial-era building that overlooks the Tonle Sap River, and admired the photographs on the wall of brave journalists who had covered the end of the Khmer Rouge regime. I ordered a beer from the horseshoe-shaped bar on the open-air terrace and then took a seat and opened my book, which was a biography of the famed journalist Martha Gellhorn, who for a time was married to Ernest Hemingway. I'd bought it the day before from a woman in Garfield pyjamas who had approached me with a stack of bootlegged books as I sat having a coffee.

As I read about how the incredible Gellhorn made it to wartime France as a stowaway on a hospital ship, I stole glances at the other patrons. The FCC, as it was known, was open to mere mortals from the public like me, but I was pretty certain that the guy sitting at the table next to mine was a journalist, absorbed as he was with scribbling away in his notebook. He had dirty-blond hair, a tan as golden as an Anzac biscuit and piercing green eyes. A brown leather satchel lay open on the lounge next to him, with half a packet of cigarettes, a lighter and a few pens strewn across the cushion. To my dismay, after about fifteen minutes he suddenly packed up his things and left, having never so much as glanced in my direction. I sighed dreamily as his broad shoulders disappeared out of sight, wondering what exciting journalistic mission he had set off on.

I sure had a thing for journalists.

My ex-boyfriend Matthew had been a senior news producer at the ABC. I looked up to him as if he were some kind of god. He was also ridiculously gorgeous, and eleven years older than me. He lived in a new apartment near the city. I lived with my parents in the sticks. I'd moved back home in order to save up for my trip and would stay at Matthew's place on the weekends.

I kept reading at the FCC until it was almost time for dinner, and then wandered out to the street. Phnom Penh was like one big, open-air restaurant. I was eating virtually all my meals on the street and loving the new taste sensations. In less than a week I'd eaten more noodles than I had over the course of the previous year. Another immediate favourite was the spicy barbecued chicken from the vendor opposite the guesthouse – the night before I'd bought a whole chook for seventy cents and split it with the owner's son, who was the guy who had checked me in. I was eating like a king and paying peanuts, and in an email to Mum and Dad that morning I'd told them that I was pleased with how well I was maintaining my budget and finding my groove as a backpacker.

I ambled down a bustling side street, where the smells of fried garlic and galangal wafted my way. Piled up on large metal trays were crickets, snails, speckled quail eggs, shiny black beetles and silkworms plump with larvae. A wok embedded in the cart was filled to the brim with dark-brown oil and floating crickets.

The man slowly stirring the bubbling concoction smiled at me and said, 'Would you like to try some crickets?'

I gulped, shook my head and continued walking. I passed a small stall that specialised in long-beaked baby birds. Their crispy skin was as red as a chicken tandoori. The stall next to it sold what I assumed were eels. Their taut bodies had been curled into S-shapes and impaled onto wooden skewers.

'Hi, Miss. You want to try some?' asked the female vendor, using a set of tongs to turn one of the creatures over so that I could see its underbelly. 'Look – it is a very tasty snake.'

I smiled nervously and backed away, unsure that such a thing existed.

The Cambodian people experienced years of famine during the 1970s and had to resort to eating whatever they could to survive. High rates of poverty and malnutrition persist to the present day, which means that cheap sources of protein like snakes and creepy-crawlies remained on the menu.

Despite knowing this, my mouth dropped open when I reached the last stall. There on display in a huge metal tray were deep-fried tarantulas. There were hundreds of them – maybe even a thousand. They were as black as night and looked as though they had been dipped in a sticky tar. They had swollen abdomens and long, hairy legs – which I expected to start moving any second. It suddenly occurred to me that if these were the cooked ones – where did they keep the ones still alive? I didn't stick around long enough to find out.

I was eager to sample as much local fare as possible and so far I had been delighted by Khmer cuisine, with its delicate, coconut-based curries and the liberal use of a fermented fish paste called *prahok*. But I wasn't sure if I could bring myself to try these more exotic offerings. It was so counter-intuitive to touch a spider or a snake – let alone put one inside my mouth and swallow it. Of course, I knew they were dead and that my fears weren't rational. Could I possibly overcome them?

Start off slow. Work your way up the food chain, I told myself.

I strolled back to the man with the crickets. He sold me a bag of ten for 1000 riels, which was about thirty cents.

'Do I just, uh, put it in my mouth?' I asked him.

'No,' he replied, laughing. 'Like this. First, rip off the tail. Then the legs.' He plucked them off neatly between his thumb and forefinger and flicked them onto the ground. 'I like to take off the head, but that's up to you,' he added, before popping the decapitated cricket into his mouth.

I copied what he'd shown me, feeling a little self-conscious. I crunched slowly on the cricket. It wasn't an offensive flavour – it sort of tasted like seaweed, with seasoning that was a little sweet. But the texture was weird to me – almost like straw. I was pleased to have tried crickets, but I gave the remaining eight to my cyclo driver on the way back to the guesthouse.

With my confidence growing about what I was willing to try, for dinner the following night I ate a plate of sautéed frogs. Funnily enough, they tasted a lot like chicken, only a tad blander, and there were lots of tiny bones to navigate. In fact, they made for an insubstantial meal and I started feeling hungry again not long afterwards. By ten o'clock, I couldn't ignore my growling stomach. I folded the page of my book to mark where I was, and then swapped my boxer shorts for my fisherman pants, which I fastened with a quick fold and a knot of the drawstring.

Even at this hour, I didn't have to walk far to find delicious street eats. If anything, the number of street-food stalls seemed to multiply at night. I walked past another couple of guest-houses, a pharmacy and a bank with a security guard nodding off on a chair, his AK-47 slung casually across his lap. Then I came to a small collection of barbecue stalls that were emanating a tantalising smell and a serious amount of smoke. I sidled up to the first one, where a man was immersed in carefully rotating skewered drumsticks, chicken feet, walnut-sized balls of pork and thickly seasoned strips of lamb. The fatty meats sizzled and popped over a bed of charcoal. Once a skewer of meat was cooked through, he transferred it to a large metal platter. In the middle of the platter were half a dozen oversized eggs.

I settled on the lamb strips and as the vendor was slipping them into a freezer bag, I noticed that one of the eggs had half its shell removed. It was no ordinary boiled egg. A thick brown vein cut through liquid swirls of blue and grey. I immediately recognised it as a duck fetus. Incredible! I knew about this unusual Southeast Asian snack because my favourite manager at the publishing company in Melbourne had raved about it. Ira's family was from the Philippines, another country where the delicacy can be found. I knew that she would be mightily impressed if I told her I had tried it.

I asked the man to add a duck fetus to my order, and he happily popped it in another freezer bag along with a slice of lemon and sachets of salt and pepper. Excited, I took the two bags back to my room. I put a towel on the bed so that I didn't dirty the sheets and then laid out the food on top.

I knew I had to eat the duck fetus quickly, or else risk losing my nerve. But first I devoured the lamb; it was salty, tender and completely delicious. Next I tapped the eggshell on the bed frame and peeled off the top to take a closer look. A clear liquid oozed out of the shell and dripped onto the towel. It had a strange, unfamiliar smell. The fetus was encased in a transparent sac, and its brown veins left an imprint on the inside of the shell. The baby duck's body was tucked up under itself, as though it were caught mid-somersault. I couldn't see its head, thankfully, as I would have felt sorry for it, although I could make out a couple of wispy feathers. I peeled off a bit more of the shell and scattered some salt and pepper over the top.

Here goes nothing.

I took a bite and instinctively closed my eyes. It was so slimy. It had the texture of silken tofu and a flavour reminiscent of chicken soup and something fermented. I chewed quickly and willed myself to take a second bite. I couldn't finish it and I'd never do it again, but I was happy to have tried duck fetus. With a satisfied sigh, I resumed my book before switching off the light twenty minutes later. I lay in the dark, happily thinking about the email I would send to Ira the following day and the group email that would soon follow it. Matthew would see that I was more adventurous than he realised.

But no sooner had I started to compile a few sentences in my head than I began to feel strange. At first it was just an overly full feeling, and I wondered if my late supper had been too big to digest. I shuddered as a wave of nausea passed through me before I broke out in a clammy sweat. Something inside me was extremely uncomfortable, but I couldn't pinpoint where. I just had a growing sense of wanting to be rid of something.

Then I leaned over the side of my bed and vomited. I hauled

myself into the bathroom, where I continued to be violently sick. As the pain ratcheted up and I emptied what felt like my entire insides, it crossed my mind that I may need to go to hospital. Frightened and groaning, I sat slumped on the toilet, begging for it to end. At various times I tried crawling back into bed, only to have to return, again and again, to the bathroom. Thank goodness I hadn't taken a third bite – assuming it was the fetus and not the meat that was making me sick. For the following few hours I was lost in a stupor of pain, sweats and nausea.

When I opened my eyes, I had no idea what time it was, though it was still completely dark. I immediately sensed that something was very wrong. I was lying on my bed, but my lower half felt drenched, as though I were in a bath. Had I wet myself? Oh my god: the stench. It was worse than that. Far, far worse.

With hiccupping sobs, I took off my soiled clothes and stuffed them in my wash bag. So much for trying to keep the bedsheet clean with a towel when I ate the duck fetus the night before – the putrid mess would have stained through to the mattress. I had to leave the guesthouse right away: the smell was too intense to bear. I felt terrible for whoever opened the door in the morning and had to literally deal with my shit. At least I'd already paid for the night in advance. Feeling dizzy and weak, I pulled on my backpack, gently closed the door behind me and slipped out.

I took a cab to Monivong Boulevard and checked into a budget high-rise hotel. As dawn broke outside and the hubbub of street commerce began, I lay miserably on the starched white sheets. I was still up and down to the toilet and had constant pins and needles, but I was fairly sure that I had passed through the worst of it.

I didn't leave the hotel room for two days. I was relieved to at least be somewhere comfortable to recover. I kept the thick drapes closed and was forever adjusting the air conditioning to manage my sweats and chills. In between napping, I listlessly watched cable TV shows and sipped the hydration salts I'd packed in my first-aid kit. I ordered honey toast from room service, but just the sight of it sent me back to the toilet. In fact, the nausea kicked in every time I thought of anything that was new to me: the streets, the heat, the language, and definitely the food and the smells. I was weepy and terribly homesick. I felt wretched about having a year of travelling ahead of me. All I wanted was my mum.

I thought over and over about how foolish I'd been. In trying to save money by only eating street food, I'd made myself sick and was blowing my budget on a hotel room.

Well played, idiot.

By the third day, I felt I could brave the outside world again. I put on a pair of noticeably looser jeans shorts and stepped out onto the balcony. Once my eyes had adjusted to the blinding sunlight, I saw a fast-food shop across the street selling chicken and chips. I didn't feel like heaving; in fact, I contemplated a serving of French fries. With joy, I realised my appetite had to be returning. But I could only stomach bland comfort food. Even the idea of noodles made me feel ill again.

When I was finally able to tell Ira that I had eaten duck fetus, and that I had never been so sick in all my life, she fired back with: 'Oh, Jess, no! Never eat duck fetus on the street. It's the sort of thing you should only have at high-end restaurants. If it's not cooked through properly, it can have some really scary bacteria. No wonder you got so sick.'

By way of a feeble reply, I admitted that I hadn't foreseen the dangers of eating street food with abandon and that, in typical Jess fashion, I had bitten off more than I could chew.

3

DARK RED ROUGE

Though I still had bouts of diarrhoea, within a few days I felt able to resume my usual sightseeing activities. I hopped on a motorcycle taxi and headed for Tuol Sleng Genocide Museum. My guidebook said it was an essential place to visit in order to understand Cambodia's past. The Kiwi couple, Deb and Phil, had told me it was pretty intense, and from the name alone, I knew that it wouldn't be easy viewing. Even so, I was completely unprepared for the experience.

I was dropped off out the front of the building, which was in a quiet residential neighbourhood. I bought a ticket and strolled into what appeared at first glance to be an ordinary high school. In the middle of the school was a pleasant, well-tended grassy area dotted with tall palms and tropical shrubs that were bursting with white flowers and housing a few chirping birds. Paths criss-crossed the lawn and there were several park benches. Across the grass were four identical blocks of classrooms, three storeys high and covered in black grime. Each had wide balconies, and French doors and windows with faded dusky-blue frames. As I approached the entrance to one of the buildings, I saw that barbed wire sealed off the gaps between the balconies, and iron bars were installed across every window.

I picked up a set of supplied headphones and began to listen to the audio tour. A female voice told me that after five years of civil war, a fifty-year-old man called Pol Pot came to power in 1975. He was the leader of the Communist Party, known as the Khmer Rouge, and he set about turning Cambodia into a one-party communist state. He declared the first year of his reign to be 'Year Zero', renamed the country Democratic Kampuchea, and then made money worthless and religion illegal.

Like Adolf Hitler before him, Pol Pot was a tyrannical, murderous madman. As the voice in my headphones sadly informed me, somewhere between 1.5 and 2.5 million Cambodians were murdered or died of malnutrition or a lack of basic medical care between 1975 and 1979; around a quarter of the country's population of 8 million.

Pol Pot was deeply disdainful of educated, middle-class professionals, and accused them of being disloyal when he was trying to overthrow the previous, US-backed regime. Anyone with a university degree, who spoke French or even simply wore spectacles was singled out for persecution. So were monks and ethnic minorities, who were also branded traitors.

The Khmer Rouge's top priority was increasing the output on farms. Phnom Penh and other cities were emptied of their inhabitants, who were forced to march to the countryside and become indentured labourers. Thousands died along the way. Pol Pot's catastrophically deluded vision was to re-create a society from the Middle Ages.

In 1976 the school in which I was standing had been converted into a detention centre and code-named Security Prison 21, or simply S-21. A hundred prisons like it were set up across the country, but this one became the most notorious – it was where some of the regime's most grotesque acts of genocide were committed. An estimated 14,000 to 20,000 people were imprisoned within its walls between 1976 and 1979. Only twelve survived.

Bracing myself, I walked into a former classroom. The room was bare except for a series of showcases containing black-and-white mug shots of prisoners. Around each person's neck was a piece of string with a laminated card looped through it. The prisoners were 'processed' on arrival: they were numbered, photographed and interrogated, and then forced to strip down and hand over their belongings.

I stared at the frightened and forlorn faces, and tried to put myself in their shoes. At the time these photographs were taken, an excruciating period of incarceration, torture and death awaited these people. Had they any idea what was coming?

I came to the next photo display. These showed prisoners after they had been murdered, many lying in pools of blood, some with their heads bashed in. I passed a cabinet at the back of the room filled with human skulls.

Distressed and dumbfounded, I continued into the next room. It had been roughly partitioned into rows of tiny brick cells. I peered inside one. It was more or less the width of a coffin. There was a set of leg irons bolted to the floor, which was an added cruelty in a cell that was already so tiny. I cast my mind to the inhabitants' discomfort and fear, as well as the brutal monotony of their existence: a single hour would have felt like a month.

I heard footsteps right behind me and swung around to face two guys. We exchanged weak smiles. I hadn't realised anyone else was in the room because no one spoke. My tongue felt very thick in my mouth.

I made my way into another room via a crude gap in the wall that looked as if it had been knocked out with a sledgehammer. This was where female prisoners had been kept. The dark timber cells resembled a set of narrow stables. There was a small gap in the door where a hose was inserted at intervals to wash the women as though they were farm animals.

Then I came to a room filled with macabre paintings by a prisoner called Vann Nath. He was one of the seven adults who had survived S-21: he was kept alive because his skills as a painter were deemed useful. I took a photo of a painting that depicted the sleeping arrangements in S-21. The prisoners lay on their backs in two straggly lines on the floor, crammed in like sardines. They wore nothing but shorts and were filthy, bruised, shackled and bleeding. Towards the back of the classroom lay ten small boys who were also shackled. A prison guard with a red kerchief around his neck stood over the miserable group with a whip in his hand.

The paintings made my stomach lurch. The scenes graphically depicted torture and execution, including hangings, clubbings and electric shocks. The actual instruments of torture were on display in a glass cabinet on the back wall, appearing positively medieval. I duly photographed the contents of the room, though I doubted I would ever look at them. I just felt compelled to document it.

As I crossed the courtyard to head towards a second building, I passed a young woman with frizzy blonde hair weeping on a bench. Her boyfriend sat with his arm around her, offering a tissue and looking equally shell-shocked. I then realised that what I'd initially assumed were monkey bars in the grounds were gallows.

I went up a flight of stairs and entered a room where confessions had been extracted using torture. The only furniture was a single chair and an iron bed with broken slats and bloodstains underneath. The voice on the audio tour told me that as the paranoid party leadership turned on its ranks in later years, the Khmer Rouge accused its members of spying for the CIA, KGB or neighbouring Vietnam. Entire families were brought to S-21 and executed for being so-called spies. Australian, Indian, French, British and Thai nationals were also killed after being declared enemies of the state. I was at a loss for words as I thought of the despicable acts that had taken place in the very room in which I stood.

I wandered out of the prison in a daze, having never before felt so profoundly depressed about the human species. How could we turn on each other with such savagery? When I'd learned about the Holocaust as a student, I'd attempted to comprehend it by relegating it to an earlier era, when the world was a more brutal place. But the genocide in Cambodia had happened so very recently – ending just two years before I was born.

Another distressing aspect was that justice hadn't been served. And it certainly wasn't due to a lack of evidence, as I had seen with my own eyes how the Khmer Rouge documented everything with a sickening thoroughness. Pol Pot was responsible for one of the worst mass killings of the twentieth century, yet he had lived out his life peacefully, spending just a year under house arrest following a show trial. Not long before he died in his sleep in 1998, he told an American journalist that his conscience was clear.

And why were these horrors new to me? I had only vaguely heard of Pol Pot before visiting the museum. At school, we'd never so much as spent a single class on what had happened in Cambodia. It was all the more baffling because it had occurred on Australia's doorstep.

Although I wasn't sure I could take any more, I took an auto-rickshaw to Choeung Ek, which was about fifteen kilometres away. The prisoners who hadn't been murdered within the walls of S-21 had been blindfolded and bussed there, before being executed en masse. 'Killing fields', as they came to be known, were scattered across the country.

Like S-21 prison, the site seemed innocuous at first. I could have mistaken it for a large nature reserve with plentiful trees and undulating ridges – but the ridges signified shallow mass graves. I listened to another audio tour and read the weathered timber plaques. One drew my attention to the human bones and teeth that would poke out through the earth after monsoon rains. Others indicated the number of victims thought to have been murdered in a single ditch. A glass cabinet contained the black rags the victims had been wearing. I passed a sign on a tree asking visitors to be quiet, although the request didn't seem necessary. Almost every tourist I saw was ashen-faced and silent.

I was unable to absorb the extent of the suffering the site had witnessed, let alone the rest of Cambodia. The events that took place under the Khmer Rouge represent one of the lowest points in the history of humanity. I thought of a quote by Holocaust survivor Primo Levi, whose memoir I had studied at university: 'One single Anne Frank moves us more than the countless others who suffered just as she did, but whose faces have remained in the shadows. Perhaps it is better that way; if we were capable of taking in all the suffering of all those people, we would not be able to live.'

All I could think to do was express inwardly how sorry I was to the lost souls who had died in such awful circumstances.

I am so sorry for what you had to endure. I am so, so sorry.

In all honesty, I couldn't see how it was possible for a nation to recover from something like this. The generational trauma would be passed on indefinitely.

4

MR BELLISIMO

A gaggle of backpackers were milling about the regional bus stand, either smoking, snacking or fiddling with their packs and camera gear. I was excited to be venturing beyond the capital, while also feeling sad to leave it. In a relatively short space of time, I'd become very fond of Phnom Penh.

I found the number 7 bus bay and double-checked that it was bound for the north-western town of Siem Reap, which would be my base to explore the famous temples of Angkor Wat. As I waited in line to stow my backpack, I watched a very attractive brunette hold court at the bay opposite. She wore a pair of baggy, elephant-print pants with a tight white singlet that set off a deep tan and ample cleavage. Her long hair was in a messy plait and a boxy black camera was slung across her shoulder. Three guys were nodding as she talked and laughed animatedly; they appeared completely entranced.

I showed my ticket to a wiry man, who tore off the stub and tossed my backpack into the belly of the bus, where it landed with a thump. As I was turning to leave, a girl appeared and breathlessly asked the man to retrieve her backpack.

'I can't find my passport,' she said, looking pale. 'I need to check if I put it inside my backpack.'

He complied with a grunt and began removing the bags from the cargo section. As I watched my backpack being tossed through the air a second time, I sympathised with the girl, saying how I'd almost left my passport in a café that very morning as I'd been in such a rush to make it on time. I waited with her until her bag was retrieved. She tore open the straps and zipper and ran her hand inside a side compartment. Grinning, she triumphantly waved her American passport at her boyfriend. He had been watching us from their seats with his face pressed against the window.

By the time the girl and I filed onto the bus it was full. I felt forty sets of eyeballs on me as I scoured each row for an empty seat. I was relieved to find one right up the back and continued down the aisle.

'Are you saving this seat for anyone?' I asked the guy sitting on the window side.

'Nope. It's all yours,' he replied in a thick European accent.

I gratefully slid in next to him.

'I'm Dario.'

'I'm Jess. Nice to meet you.'

Good god. In my eagerness to find a seat, I hadn't taken a proper look at the person I would be sitting next to for the next six hours. My bus-seat buddy was drop-dead gorgeous, with a chiselled jawline and skin the colour of butterscotch. He had a buzzcut, which I usually found too severe, but it accentuated his green eyes and unusually long eyelashes.

He was still smiling at me.

'I'm from Milan,' Dario said. 'Where are you from?'

Wow, Milan. One of the coolest cities in the world. His accent was beautiful. I told him that I was from Melbourne and by the time the bus lumbered out of the depot ten minutes later,

I was laughing at his anecdote about a Scottish guy on Thailand's Phi Phi Island who had drunk so many whisky cocktail buckets one night that he woke up in a canoe adrift in the ocean and had to shout at a passing boat for help.

So this adonis is funny too, I thought, and for the millionth time felt so lucky to be travelling.

As we trundled along rickety roads through lush jungle, past rice paddies, and the occasional bamboo hut and herd of water buffalo, the conversation flowed easily and the silences were comfortable when they came. Dario's iPod had broken, so we shared mine using the splitter I brought from home that connected two sets of headphones.

As we neared Siem Reap, there was no question that Dario and I would stay at the same place. We chose a guesthouse out of the listings in the *Cambodia* Lonely Planet and Dario took the room next to mine, which was on the ground floor of a three-storey block.

'I'm tired from the early start so I'm going to take a nap,' he said. 'Do you want to knock on my door later and we can grab dinner and some beers?'

Was the sky blue? Was water wet?

'That sounds great, Dario,' I said, trying to bely my eagerness.

THERE WERE ONLY a handful of other tourists at the Cambodia Landmine Museum, which was about twenty kilometres north of Siem Reap. It was an open-air museum with a few sheds facing a sickly green pond. In the middle of the pond was a glass display unit that was the size of a small hut, and it was stacked to the brim with landmines of various shapes and sizes. To me they looked innocuous; like film-reel canisters or wheel hubs. I wouldn't have thought twice about picking one up.

I read a couple of signs and learned that the mines had been laid between the 1970s and 1990s by Cambodian, Vietnamese and American forces. There were between 8 and 10 million undetonated mines scattered across the country, with the majority in the north-western region that I had arrived in. Every year, five hundred people were killed or maimed when they accidentally stepped on them. Significant chunks of land couldn't be farmed because it was too dangerous, and that left entire communities without a source of income and thus very poor. No wonder I had seen so many amputees in Phnom Penh – Cambodia has more per capita than anywhere else on earth. No wonder, either, that they had all been begging: discrimination made it next to impossible for them to find work.

I wandered over to an eerie display of stuffed mannequins. They looked like scarecrows, except they were Khmer Rouge soldiers in khaki uniforms. One was pointing a machine gun in my direction.

Nearby was a fenced enclosure that looked like an aviary. Menacing red signs featuring a skull and crossbones stated: 'Danger!! Mines!!' The warning was repeated across the top in Khmer. Another sign challenged visitors to spot the five landmines that were concealed among the dried leaves and other undergrowth inside the enclosure. I could only see two. 'Always stay on marked paths in Cambodia,' warned another sign. It was sickening to think how easy it would be to step on a mine and get blown to pieces.

Inside a shed was an art exhibition. One painting had all the hallmarks of a children's cartoon, except it depicted two boys with their arms blown off and blood spurting out, and family members standing around them wailing. Propped up against a wall were assorted prosthetic legs. They were of varying heights, depending on how much of the limb had to be amputated. A rusted cast-iron leg looked especially heavy and uncomfortable. The skin around the stump must have been rubbed red raw every time the prosthetic was worn.

There was no sign of the museum's founder, Aki Ra, who I had read about in my Lonely Planet with sad fascination. He was a former child soldier who had been forcibly conscripted to the Khmer Rouge after they murdered his parents. When the war ended, Aki Ra began the incredibly dangerous work of clearing landmines, and he adopted some of the orphans he encountered along the way. He used the proceeds from the museum to care for the orphans and to continue the mine clearing, while the museum itself spread awareness about the problem Cambodia faced.

Much like Tuol Sleng Genocide Museum, it was grim viewing. The war had ended almost thirty years ago, but the senseless deaths and horrific injuries were continuing. In all probability, a child in Cambodia had been killed or maimed that very morning while walking to school (or more likely – while walking to work).

The gift shop sold artwork and crafts made by amputees. I bought a couple of toys for my nephew Jack and some t-shirts for my sister Alice, and her husband Heath. Jack was about to turn one, so I got him a plush turtle and a Cambodia onesie. I thought sadly of the disparity between the life opportunities Jack had in Australia in comparison with the person who made the toys. He or she would be lucky to make a dollar a day. It was such an unfair world.

I WAS RUNNING low on riel, so on my way back to the guesthouse I asked the tuktuk driver to drop me off at Old Market, which in

Khmer was called Pshar Chas. I fronted up to a little counter on the perimeter and handed over one hundred and fifty Australian dollars. In exchange I was given nearly half a million riel.

I've never felt so wealthy in all my life, I thought as I stuffed the wads of cash into my bumbag, which I wore on the inside of my trousers with my passport every day.

I went inside the market to grab a snack that I could take back to my room. I walked past a couple of fabric stores, a pungent fishmonger's and a shop with a dozen varieties of rice that could be scooped out of open hessian bags. Next to a tall pile of watermelons was a bench laden with bunches of lychees, bananas, pomegranates and mangos. A long papaya had been split open down the middle to reveal its plump black seeds. I haggled over a bunch of bananas, and when I smiled and said 'som', which is Khmer for 'please', the woman beamed and immediately halved the price. I handed over the equivalent of five cents. I still couldn't get over how cheap everything was.

I found myself in the cured-sausage section, where I gazed up at a row of pigs' heads hanging off metal hooks. Their eyes were open, their ears cocked and they were actually smiling. In fact, they didn't look at all dead, which was disconcerting.

I spun round when someone tapped me on the shoulder. A young woman – a girl, really – was carrying a baby in a sling. It lay there limp and naked, without even a nappy. Its eyes were caked together with muck and its tiny chest rose and fell with shallow breaths.

'My baby is sick. It needs milk formula. But I have no money. Please can you buy me some formula?'

'Of course,' I said, alarmed. The baby looked as though it were on death's door. I wasn't even sure if a trip to hospital could save it, let alone a bit of milk.

'Thank you so much,' said the young mother quietly. 'Please, follow me.'

We wove our way through the labyrinth of stores until we came to a tiny shop that sold bottles of shampoo, nappies, makeup and soap. I handed over some of the riel I'd got from the money changer, and a man passed over a tin of formula.

'Thank you so much. I will take my baby home now to feed it,' said the young woman with a small smile.

'I'm glad that I could help you,' I said. 'I hope your baby feels better soon.'

As I walked outside to look for a tuktuk, it dawned on me that the reason I felt like a millionaire in Cambodia was because people like her were so poor.

※

I RETURNED to the guesthouse and knocked on Dario's door. When no answer came, I knocked again.

'Is that you, Jess? I'm coming.'

The door opened and there stood Dario, dripping wet and with nothing but a small white towel around his waist. I tried not to gape at his perfect six pack.

'Hey, Jess.' He grinned. 'I'll just throw on some clothes. Give me two minutes, okay?'

'Sure.'

I trailed after Dario up to the rooftop bar, catching whiffs of his cologne that was like a fresh ocean spray. We chose a seat on a rattan sofa with faded green cushions and Dario went off to the bar to get us a drink. I sat back and drank in my surrounds. Travellers were laughing and playing pool or chatting on lounges. The sun was beginning to set and a warm breeze ruffled the tropical pot plants, which seemed to sway in time to the rhythm of the Bob Marley album being played. A blackboard advertised beers at just fifty cents a glass and a daily happy hour that lasted four hours. Plates of food were arriving on a pulley from the kitchen that was located on ground level – it was like something out of Enid Blyton's *The Faraway Tree*. My life was officially magical.

Dario and I hadn't been talking long when a guy came and sat down on the sofa opposite us and introduced himself as Justin. He was also from Melbourne, which was exciting for me. He looked a bit like Kurt Cobain, with unkempt blond hair, stubble and intense blue eyes. I looked back and forth at the two hotties and almost started laughing.

My friends tried to tell me there were plenty more fish in the sea.

I told Dario and Justin about the sick baby at the market.

'Oh, apparently that's a scam,' said Justin. 'I overheard a girl yesterday telling the guesthouse manager the exact same story. He told her that the woman would be in cahoots with the shop owner, and they would split the money you paid for the formula – which would have been five times the usual price. The baby probably wasn't even hers.'

'Oh.' I was so shocked that at first I couldn't think of anything else to say. 'But the baby really did look sick,' I added.

Justin shrugged. 'It probably was. That's the girl over there – her name is Lucy. You could go ask her about it.'

I left the guys to chat and went to introduce myself to Lucy. Sure enough, she'd had the exact same experience as me, although she had paid a few dollars less for the formula.

'It feels crap to know I was ripped off, but I'm also sad that I haven't actually found a way to help anyone,' I said. 'I wish there was something I could do. I feel bad just being here and having a good time while Cambodians face such a struggle with everyday life.'

'You could volunteer as an English-language teacher,' Lucy replied. 'I was going to do it, but I've got to meet a friend in Battambang by Friday. Volunteering as a teacher is better than giving people money. That way you're giving them a skill, rather than encouraging them to beg because it's lucrative,' she said. 'I'll introduce you to Saki. She teaches Japanese at a local school.'

I wasn't sure if I agreed with Lucy's theory. Surely people only turned to begging if they had no other alternative and had hit absolute rock bottom.

All the same, I went to speak to Saki about volunteering at the school. I told her that I didn't have a teaching degree or anything – I was a law graduate who had never practiced. I just knew that I wanted to help. She laughed and said she had a commerce degree, but here she was in Cambodia. I liked her immediately. She was bubbly and sweet, and wore a funky, loose-fitting denim dress over candy-striped bike shorts. She invited me to watch her next class and promised to introduce me to one of the school's organisers.

I returned to Dario and Justin, who were chatting to a sunburned German couple. Dario smiled when he saw me and shifted over to make space next to him on the couch. A couple of minutes later, he rested his hand on my thigh and gave it a small squeeze. It felt as if an electric current passed through my body. I couldn't concentrate on what the others were saying, so I just grinned and nodded vacuously.

A couple of hours later, we headed back to our rooms after arranging to meet Justin the next morning so that we could split the cost of a tuktuk while exploring the temples together. Dario and I walked along a pebbled path until we came to our block of rooms. Green tree frogs were hopping across the smooth tiled walkway and making a din with their croaking. A couple of bats swooshed overhead through the starry sky. It was a beautifully still, hot night.

'That's a big one,' said Dario, pointing to a massive gecko on the wall near the lamplight, its tongue swishing at mosquitoes.

'He's a beefcake,' I replied.

'Tomorrow will be great,' he said.

'I can't wait.'

We stood there smiling at one another. Dario was so close that I could feel his breath on my face. He leaned in to kiss me and I closed my eyes. He was a very good kisser.

'Would you like to come inside?' he asked. His arm was around my waist and our bodies were touching, as though we were about to start slow dancing.

I nodded. Of course I wanted to. But I hadn't been with anyone since Matthew. Would it mess with my head or help me to get over him?

There was only one way to find out.

WHEN I OPENED my eyes the next morning, the first thing I saw was Dario's bare shoulders. As I watched the gentle rise and fall of his breath, I thought about the last time I'd woken up next to Matthew. It was a painful, yet exquisite memory. We had got tangled up in the sheets, so to speak, and he had almost been late to work at the ABC. Without even time for a shower, he had thrown on a t-shirt hanging over a chair and leaned down to kiss me goodbye.

'Stay as long as you want. There's breakfast stuff in the fridge. See ya, beautiful.'

Matthew always called me that: never by my name. He always kissed me with a luscious urgency, and he always seemed glad to see me. But he never told me that he loved me. After we'd been dating a few months, I couldn't hold in my feelings anymore, and I blurted out that I was in love with him. He looked at me for a few seconds with a shocked expression, and I thought I was going to die of embarrassment. He changed the subject. He broke up with me a week later, saying that his feelings weren't as strong as mine. The heartache was excruciating.

Dario rolled over to face me. He smiled and I thought once again how handsome he was. Lying next to him was like being in a scene from a movie with a heartthrob actor.

'Good morning, Jess,' he said, drawing me into his arms and nuzzling my neck. 'How did you sleep?'

'Perfectly,' I mumbled happily.

And then his lips were on mine and I could no longer recall the past.

5

THE LOST KINGDOM

Even from a distance, the sight of Angkor Wat filled my heart with its breathtaking beauty. The ancient temple was perfectly symmetrical and utterly enormous: it towered over the jungle landscape we'd been travelling through in a tuktuk. Angkor Wat's silhouette of five pine-cone-shaped towers was already familiar to me because it was Cambodia's national symbol and adorned everything from the flag to the currency and bottles of Angkor beer. To see it in real life, with its reflection mirrored in a huge moat, was nothing short of captivating.

Dario, Justin and I clambered out of the tuktuk and joined the throng of tourists heading towards the causeway. A lilting instrumental performance grew louder as we approached a fig tree with a broad canopy. A band of six sat under its shade on a couple of bamboo mats, with their crutches lying beside them. They were yet more landmine victims. I dropped a 5000-riel note into an upturned baseball cap in front of a man playing the lute, who smiled and nodded his thanks.

A few seconds later, I felt a tugging on my t-shirt. I looked down and saw a little girl staring up at me with pleading eyes.

'Please, Miss,' she said as she held out an empty milk bottle. A baby was asleep inside a chequered cloth sling that was fastened to her hip. I shook my head and kept walking. It was probably a scam, but I felt stingy and miserable all the same. Sensing my internal conflict, Dario smiled at me sadly.

It was only 9:30 am, but the sun's rays were fierce and I was pouring sweat as we walked across the paved, stone causeway. Dario was sweating too, but he somehow just looked sexy; like a soccer player striding off the pitch. Justin joked that the moat on either side of us was so inviting he was going to jump in.

After passing through a stone entrance that looked like a gigantic picture frame, the moat ended and on either side of the footbridge was an expanse of lawn that I figured would have been pleasure gardens. Dotted about were smaller temples and a couple of ponds. I saw a tourist riding a pony with a tasselled bridle and made a mental note to do the same on our way out.

There were so many tourists that we had to queue at a set of steps that led up to the inner chamber of the temple. There was a sense of excited anticipation in the air and I loved trying to guess the different accents and languages I could hear. Directly in front of us was a North American couple who were probably retirees. They were both quite overweight. The wife had a syrupy accent and a voice that could project across an auditorium with ease. Ahead of them was a pair of stunning French girls, both blonde, who looked as if they had stepped off the set of a shampoo commercial. I recognised a lanky man who had overtaken us with his loping stride a few minutes earlier. He was poring over a map. A group of six Chinese tourists with red stickers on their t-shirts were chatting away animatedly with their guide, who wore a sun visor and golf shorts.

'Did you know that in China, you only get five days of holiday a year?' said Justin quietly.

'No way,' I said. 'How is it even possible to travel in such a short space of time?'

'Well, they have to move really fast and pack everything in. That's why you often see them on tours. So they don't waste any time.'

'I'd hate that,' I said. I wasn't sure if even a whole year of travelling would be enough for me.

We were soon happily lost inside the temple's vast network of chambers and passageways, which extended up into the second and third floors. It was so big that for the most part it didn't feel as though it were crawling with tourists – and sometimes we had parts of it to ourselves. As we walked along a palatial hall, I traced my finger over bas-reliefs – carvings of voluptuous deities projected out of the walls. In a shadowy passageway, we came upon a monk praying quietly as he sat cross-legged, his orange robe folded neatly around his ankles. Thin trails of smoke rose from sticks of incense and were illuminated by a beam of sunshine streaming in through a window. It was incredibly atmospheric; a photographer's paradise.

After exploring a central courtyard, we climbed a set of incredibly steep steps to the top of the central tower, which my guidebook informed me was twice the height of the Tower of London. Dario offered his hand to steady me as I came up off the last step. The view was magnificent.

'How on earth did they build it?' I marvelled. 'There weren't any cranes or trucks or anything.'

'Maybe they used elephants,' replied Dario. 'And lots of slaves. Just like they did for the Colosseum.'

Angkor Wat had been built in the twelfth century during the reign of King Suryavarman, who intended it to be his mausoleum. His wish was never fulfilled, however, as he died in a faraway battle in 1150 before his grand project had been completed. Nonetheless, by building the world's biggest religious monument, King Suryavarman was still remembered almost a thousand years after his death. He had achieved a form of immortality that I suspected he craved.

I looked at my watch and realised that we had been there for over an hour, so we returned to the carpark for a break, where we bought a few cans of Coke from a vendor sitting under an umbrella with a portable cooler box. The transaction attracted a few street kids.

'Where are you from?' asked a boy in a yellow singlet with something greasy smeared across his face.

'Australia.'

'G'day mate. Capital is Canberra. Land of the kangaroos.'

'Kangaroos,' echoed the other kids, who erupted into hysterical laughter.

'Miss, give me some money to buy pencils for school,' he said.

'Sorry – but no,' I replied firmly. I felt like an arsehole saying no to such a request, which was no doubt his intention.

The kids trailed after us as we looked for our tuktuk. At one point they were circling us like a pack of hyenas.

'Please, miss,' said the boy again, a minute later. He seemed to be the leader. 'Just give me one dollar. One dollar for me.'

I shook my head. I saw that Justin and Dario were also in the midst of a back-and-forth with other kids. They had manned up on us as if it was a game of basketball. I was relieved to finally spot our driver, who had been napping in a hammock strung up to each end of the tuktuk's roof. He told the kids to scat, although not unkindly.

'Now we will go to Angkor Thom,' he said, and with a rev of his motorbike, we left the children empty-handed in the dust.

Even with three-day passes, we would only see a fraction of the thousand or so temples at Angkor Wat, which translates to 'City of Temples' and spans an area of four hundred acres. Our tuktuk driver was a young father of twenty-six called Sok, and he had promised to show us the highlights. We had met him out the front of our guesthouse, where a dozen drivers waited for a fare every morning. Sok's English was pretty good and he was a cheerful guy. Over the hum of the diesel engine he told us he was lucky to have a job in tourism. He used to earn only thirteen dollars a month as a labour hand, which he told us was an average wage in Cambodia. But he wanted to make more money for his family, so he had started in tourism a year ago after taking some English classes. Sok told us that his father had been a teacher, before he was executed by the Khmer Rouge when Sok was a baby. A moment's shocked silence followed before we told him how sorry we were.

'It is okay,' he said sadly.

We all knew it wasn't.

ANGKOR THOM WAS SO trippy and beautiful that I wondered whether the idea for it had been dreamed up during some kind of high, whether spiritual or chemical. Sok dropped us off at the south gate, where we walked along a causeway above a moat. On either side of us were two long rows of stone figures – there must have been at least a hundred of them. To our left were placid gods, and on the right, fiery demons. The demons were holding a gigantic snake as though it were being used in a tug of war. A couple of the sculptures had a missing head or arm, but overall they were remarkably well preserved, and especially so considering how old they were. The entrance to the walled city was through imposing gates that were topped with three huge faces carved out of stone. Each was staring in a different direction, as though on permanent sentry duty.

We had almost reached the entrance when we were overtaken by a couple of tourists riding an elephant. They were sitting on a wooden platform that swayed to and fro and looked uncomfortable for them and the animal. The handler was straddled across its neck, with his legs hidden behind the floppy ears. The elephant had no harness.

'How on earth does he control it?' I wondered aloud.

'He presses his toes and heels into the ears. The skin there is really sensitive,' said Justin. 'Sometimes they use an iron hook too. It's pretty cruel.'

'Wow, man. You sure know a lot about training elephants and all kinds of other things,' said Dario.

'Yeah, well, that's because I go to the school of life,' joked Justin. 'I've been on the road for five months and I've learned a few things.'

The elephant stopped at the gate so the tourists could take photos. We walked up and patted it, and I was surprised to find that its coat was almost as rough as sandpaper. I laughed as its trunk snuffled and wriggled around my pockets in search of food.

'What a magnificent creature,' I murmured. I would have loved a ride, but it was very hot and I felt sorry for it.

Inside the walled city were yet more stone faces – at Bayon Temple, which was smack bang in the middle, there were hundreds of them. They peered down at us from the tops of towers with a serene, knowing gaze. Each face was so big that a single boulder constituted just half a lip or a nostril.

We were exploring a temple decorated with three-headed elephants when a monkey suddenly leaped out at us. I jumped a mile and it narrowly missed Dario's head before scampering off into the foliage.

'I feel like I'm Indiana Jones on a jungle quest,' joked Dario.

And you're just as handsome as he is.

Angkor Thom was created during the rule of King

Jayavarman VII, who was the empire's first Buddhist king after centuries of Hindu leaders. The royal city flourished for three hundred years, until one ill-fated day during the fifteenth century when forces from the rival Ayutthaya Kingdom in Siam (which is in modern-day Thailand) invaded and drove out its inhabitants. No one ever lived there again and the Khmer empire collapsed.

As we were hurtling along an asphalt track in the tuktuk, we spotted a few kids swimming in a large dam known as East Baray. Justin asked Sok to stop for a few minutes.

'Come on – let's have a swim!' said Justin. With a grin, he waded in.

I thought about it for a second, and then followed him. I was fully clothed, but it was so hot that my t-shirt and shorts would dry quickly. Dario shook his head at us, laughing, and took a few photos. Then he peeled off his t-shirt and jumped in too. The kids didn't ask us for anything as we splashed around with them. It was really nice.

Dripping wet and refreshed, we devoured plates of noodles with shredded cabbage and a spicy-sweet sauce from an eatery under a green tarpaulin. We chatted away like old friends. Dario was affectionate, but he didn't come off as intense. To my surprise, neither did I. It was very different from being with Matthew, which had been painful from the beginning because I was so in love with him and sensed his feelings lacked the same intensity. Being with Dario felt easy and fun, and I liked that he gave me confidence rather than draining my existing supplies.

As soon as I laid eyes on Ta Prom's otherworldly, ethereal beauty, I knew it was my favourite temple. The others had been carefully restored upon their rediscovery, but this one had been left exactly as it lay during those three centuries of abandonment after the Khmer empire fell. The local population had known of Angkor Wat's existence all along, but a French naturalist called Henri Mouhot is credited for bringing the temples to the attention of the international community in 1860 after he made what must have been an utterly jaw-dropping discovery.

The jungle had reclaimed much of Ta Prom. Exposed roots of strangler figs had grown up and over it, which created the impression of the structure being cradled by giant hands. Broken boulders lay across the path and flaxen witch's hair lichen dangled from branches overhead. A thick coating of electric-green moss covered much of the ruins. I had never seen such an exquisite blending of the natural and manmade environments.

Ta Prom had been nicknamed the 'Tomb Raider Temple' because scenes from the blockbuster Hollywood movie with Angelina Jolie had been filmed there a few years earlier. I hadn't seen *Tomb Raider*, but it was easy to visualise Lara Croft leaping over the tree roots with a pistol in a holster and her long plait swinging behind her.

Sok then took us to the hot-air-balloon station, which we were excited about because none of us had been on one before. But my heart sank when I saw a group of beggars standing around in front of the ticket office. There was a street kid who was also an amputee – his missing leg replaced by a single crutch. He'd never had a chance in life, I sadly surmised. And yet when the boy hopped over to me, I heard myself refusing to give him any money. I wanted to, but I was scared that if I did the other beggars would swoop in like seagulls. So I shook my head again and kept walking. I wasn't indifferent to the boy's plight, but he wouldn't know it from my cold demeanour.

Although we were millionaires in comparison with the locals outside the ticket booth, Dario, Justin and I could not have afforded the cost of a real balloon ride. However, this one had been specifically adapted for backpacker budgets. The balloon was not the usual teardrop shape, but instead resembled a gigantic yellow beach ball. And instead of a basket underneath was a donut-shaped metal platform, where a few tourists had assembled before take-off. There was no burner inside it either. It was tethered to the ground with wires, so the balloon went straight up and down rather than drifting across the sky. It cost five dollars for a ten-minute ride.

With a heave and a wobble, the balloon took off. Up into the sky we went, grinning and holding onto the side bars. I felt a bit giddy as I looked at the ground getting further away. Only rope netting prevented us from falling out.

From a higher vantage point, I was better able to absorb the scale of the historic site and its design. Angkor Wat had been built on a piece of land that looked like a gigantic computer chip, with the absolutely massive moat surrounding it. All the right angles were incredibly precise, which was itself a remarkable feat of pre-industrial engineering. The tourists traversing the causeway looked like ants, and it occurred to me that the moment in time in which I was looking at them was microscopic. What was a single day in the span of the nine hundred years that had passed since the temple was built?

I was gazing out at an empire that was once the most powerful and sophisticated in the world. In 1400, when London had a middling population of 50,000, the kingdom of Angkor had more than a million inhabitants and a territory that stretched from Vietnam to Brunei. It had flourished for six hundred years, from the ninth to the fifteenth centuries.

But somehow Cambodia had become one of the world's poorest countries, and surely the most traumatised too, following a recent war and genocide. I knew that when we came back down to the ground, there would be a collection of ragtag street kids and downtrodden beggars desperately hoping for our spare change. It was difficult to reconcile the grandeur of Cambodia's past with its heartbreaking present in the twenty-first century. How did a country's fortunes change so dramatically? Could the situation ever be turned around?

As some of the sun's intensity began to dissipate in the afternoon, the three of us explored some of the smaller, less crowded temples. We were padding along a shadowy chamber of a particularly peaceful temple when I felt a sudden quickening in my bowels. I urgently needed a toilet, and with a panicked feeling I realised we were a long way from any public facilities. I still hadn't fully recovered from the duck-fetus incident and it seemed that the Imodium tablet I had taken for the bus journey to Siem Reap had worn off. Or maybe something I'd eaten at lunch hadn't agreed with me.

'I've got to go to the toilet,' I muttered to Justin and Dario, and scampered off before they had time to reply.

I nipped out a side exit and down a few stairs, then raced around the side path that lined the temple's perimeter. I stopped when I spotted a large tree a few metres away. It would give me some privacy to relieve myself. But between me and the tree was the same innocuous-looking foliage that I'd seen at the landmine museum when I was warned never to stray from a marked path. As horrified as I was by the idea of doing a poo in public view, getting blown up was unquestionably worse.

Oh god.

I hurriedly pulled out the roll of toilet paper I kept in my bag and crouched down. I was on an awkward angle, with my bum backed up disrespectfully onto the outer edge of the temple and my feet facing the tree trunk. As I was doing the unthinkable on a wonder of the ancient world, I heard a sound that made my heart stop: laughter. Tourists were approaching along a passageway inside the temple. Would they see me? I couldn't bear the idea of our eyes meeting, so I looked down at the ground and counted to ten as my cheeks burned with shame. When I dared to look up again, the chatter had died away. I finished my business and returned red-faced to Dario and Justin.

'All okay, Jess?' Dario asked me.

'Yep, fine,' I replied with a forced smile. I wanted to get out of there as quickly as possible. 'Let's head to the next temple.'

As we started walking back towards Sok at the tuktuk, I couldn't help but wonder whether I was going to spend the next year pooping in all the wrong places. It was a mortifying prospect. I was beginning to realise that travelling could be totally amazing and intensely uncomfortable – all within the space of a day.

6

HAVE BACKPACK, WILL TEACH

Dario and I spent our last afternoon together relaxing on the rooftop of the three-storey building our rooms were in. I'd discovered it by chance the day before when I'd walked to the top of the stairs to see where they led. It had a nice view of the patchwork of buildings below and we had it all to ourselves.

Dario and I stretched out on towels and listened to Nina Simone singing and the bullfrogs croaking. We talked about how amazing Angkor Wat had been, and all the places we wanted to see in the world. It was incredibly humid and when the skies suddenly opened and let forth a torrential downpour, we took it as a sign that it was time for Dario to start thinking about heading to the bus station.

I sat on the end of his bed and watched him pack as I absent-mindedly twisted the frizzy tendrils that formed around my forehead whenever it rained. He rolled his t-shirts and shorts into neat little sausage shapes and placed them side-by-side in his pack. He sniffed a t-shirt that had been draped over a chair, and then added it to the contents of his wash bag. Then he took a swig of water and swallowed a couple of paracetamol.

'Hurting a lot?' I asked over the pounding of the rain.

'Yeah, it is,' he said, rubbing his jaw.

Dario's toothache had begun about a week ago and it had become so painful he could no longer ignore it. After taking the overnight bus to Bangkok he would see a dentist in the morning. Bangkok was the best place to get medical treatment in Southeast Asia because it was cheap but standards were world class. From there he planned to head south towards Malaysia. Justin had left the day before for the beaches of Sihanoukville. I was staying on in Siem Reap to teach some English classes, and would then slowly make my way north to Laos. Our happy trio was no more.

Dario zipped up his backpack, attached a snug waterproof cover and then hoisted it onto his back. He fastened the waist strap with a click, then cinched it tight. I got up off the bed.

'Bye, Jess,' he said, cupping my chin. 'I'll email you from Bangkok. I hope that we'll meet again one day.'

'It's been amazing to have met you,' I replied.

He kissed me one last time and then he disappeared out the door and into the rain.

I DIDN'T FEEL like being alone, so I went straight up to the rooftop restaurant and ordered a beer and a comfort meal of spaghetti bolognese. The rain soon stopped and everything looked refreshed and was bathed in a golden evening glow. But the backpackers I met I didn't much like, which did nothing to help my fragile mood. I found myself sitting at a table with a British guy in an Angkor beer singlet who was bragging about how he'd paid his tuktuk driver just a dollar to take him around Angkor Wat. That seemed to egg on the girl next to him to tell us how she and her pal had that day saved fifty cents on their tuktuk fare back from the market.

'I said to him, "What are you going to do if we don't pay the full price? It's not our fault you don't have change." And then we just got out and walked off!'

The British guy and the girl laughed.

I found them repellent, but I stayed quiet. I wasn't in the mood for an argument. Then a blonde Irish girl with heavy eyeliner and boobs bulging out of a white crop-top arrived and started hitting on the British guy. He was attractive in a preppy way, but he was a total douche bag. She was laughing loudly at his bad jokes and would feign indignation and slap him on the thigh when he teased her.

Ugh, gross.

I was about to go back to my room and turn in early with a book when a Canadian guy called Pete came and took a seat next to me, and we started chatting. Pete had been travelling for three months across Southeast Asia and he was about to go on tour back in Canada with his indie band, the Belushis. He told me all about Ratanakiri province, where he had just returned from. He had ridden elephants along red-dirt tracks and washed them in a raging river that was deep within the jungle. He swam at a pristine waterfall and slept in a hut with a Cambodian family.

'It sounds amazing,' I said.

'And there are hardly any tourists there because it's pretty remote,' he replied.

'That sounds like an added bonus,' I said. I gave a little nod in the direction of the Irish girl, who was by this time sitting on the British guy's lap and ruffling his hair while undoubtedly giving him a massive boner.

Pete laughed. 'Well anyhow, tonight is my last night so I want to do something memorable,' he said. 'I was thinking of going to a nightclub – not one that's geared towards Westerners, but where the locals go to party.'

'That sounds fun,' I said. 'I'll come with you.'

We downed our beers and jumped in a tuktuk.

It took a bit of time to make the driver understand that we weren't looking for a nightclub oriented towards backpackers. At the second place he took us to, Pete rejected it by saying, 'No – Khmer party.'

'Ah – okay, okay,' said the driver. He did a U-turn away from the tourist strip and within five minutes he'd dropped us at a nondescript building with a few people standing out the front. The lack of flashing neon signs in English looked promising, so we paid him and got out.

I felt the vibrations of the thumping base reverberate through me as we approached the building. An unsmiling security guard pointed us down a set of stairs. We came out onto a packed dance floor that was completely dark in between the flashes of strobe and pulsing lasers. Pete's white t-shirt was glowing fluorescent purple in the dark. His teeth were purple too. We found the bar and ordered a couple of tequila shots for a dollar each.

'Ready for the lick, sip, suck?' I asked Pete as I dabbed a bit of salt on my wrist before handing him the shaker.

We licked the salt, shot the tequila and sucked the lemon. Grinning, we moved out onto the dance floor. For a few seconds, Pete pretended to do air guitar with a head-banging motion, which totally didn't go with the electronica and made me laugh. We seemed to be the only Westerners there, but no one looked particularly surprised to see us. A couple of girls smiled at me, but most people didn't pay us any attention. I could tell from the way people were dressed that this was where the rich kids came to play. Pete and I looked pretty scruffy by comparison.

We went back to the bar and ordered a second round of

tequila shots. I was grimacing from the sour lemon and bitter tequila when a guy sidled over to us. He wore an open black shirt with a gold cross on a chain. He introduced himself as 'the Boss' and told us that was what everyone called him. He wasn't joking. Two guys and a very beautiful girl with long black hair stood half a step behind him, nodding as he spoke. His entourage, I assumed.

We made small talk for a couple of minutes before the Boss asked if we'd like to do karaoke.

'Great idea!' I shouted over the music, despite the fact that I couldn't sing to save myself.

Needless to say, Pete was more than qualified to pick up a microphone and didn't need any convincing.

We followed the Boss down a corridor that opened up into a smoky lounge with another bar. The guys were choosing a bottle of whisky when I noticed a window in the wall. It struck me as odd because the rest of the place had no windows, so I strolled over to it. Twenty or so young women were sitting on rows of bleachers. At first I thought it was double-sided glass, because they seemed oblivious to me staring at them. A few of the girls were chatting to one another, but they mostly just sat there looking bored. They wore skimpy singlets and barely-there miniskirts or hot pants with stilettos. Pinned to their chests was a laminated card with a number on it, which made me think of the prisoners in the black-and-white photos at the genocide museum in Phnom Penh. I realised these girls were prostitutes who could be bought like cattle at an auction.

I went back to the group and we settled into our karaoke room, which had a couple of old vinyl couches and a big TV. There were sodas and bags of chips and peanuts, and a thick catalogue of songs to choose from. Pete belted out a Matchbox Twenty song without needing to read the lyrics that appeared across the bottom of the screen. A saccharine video clip featured a couple holding hands on the beach and the guy later staring at the rain after some kind of misunderstanding. The Boss and his buddies sang some Khmer romantic pop hits, as did the beautiful girl, who was otherwise quite shy. I massacred a Madonna song. Pete and the Boss sung Ricky Martin's 'Livin' La Vida Loca' with a lot of energy and hip thrusting. Pete had me in stitches. But I couldn't stop thinking about those girls in the fishbowl of a room. Having them on display like that was so clinical. It struck me that unless it was a sporting team, putting numbers on people was a terrible idea.

I GROANED when the alarm went off at seven the next morning. I would have rolled over and gone straight back to sleep, but I had to meet Saki for breakfast. She was taking me to the languages school an hour before her Japanese class started so I could watch an English lesson being taught. As I had no teaching experience, Saki said this would help me plan my first lesson for the following day.

On our way to the classroom, we popped into the manager's office so I could introduce myself. Angela was from Seattle and she had been living in Cambodia for the past two years. She seemed so confident and at ease in her surroundings, and when a cleaner stopped by with a mop and bucket, Angela switched to speaking in Khmer. I listened in awe.

Saki and I headed to the classroom and took the only seats left, which were right up the back. There were about twenty kids aged between seven and twelve, and they were chattering away with the kind of excitement I'd expect to see at a birthday party. The walls were covered with colourful world maps, pictures of animals, numbers and the alphabet. A light breeze blew in through the open windows and a ceiling fan whirred overhead.

As the hands on the clock at the front of the classroom read ten past eight, the teacher was still nowhere to be seen. My hangover was moving into a deeper phase, with a somersaulting stomach that kept crying out for something fried and salty, even though I'd had a massive breakfast. At a quarter past eight, Angela poked her head through the classroom door.

'Jess, it looks as though the teacher isn't coming. Can you teach your first lesson today?'

'But I haven't prepared anything!' I exclaimed.

'Don't worry, just make it up as you go. Some of the children travelled a long way to be here. They will be really disappointed if their class is cancelled. Unfortunately that happens more often than we'd like.'

My first reaction was to say no, but then I thought about the ragtag kids at the temples and the women with numbers pinned to their chests, and how Sok told us that his life improved when he was able to get a job in tourism after taking English classes.

'Okay sure, I'll do it,' I said, having no idea how I would.

'Thanks a bunch,' said Angela, before ducking back into the corridor.

I walked to the front of the classroom. Saki gave me an encouraging smile.

'Right,' I began, a little tentatively. 'My name is Jessica and I am from Australia. I will teach you today.' I looked around the room for inspiration. 'Can anyone point to their nose?'

Twenty hands whipped to the tip of their noses.

'Excellent,' I said. 'Who can point to their eyes? Great. Ears? Hair? You're good! I'll have to make this harder.'

We moved on to nostril, pimple, mole, eyelash and eyebrow. When I ran out of body parts, we got started on words about cooking, because I couldn't stop thinking about food. At one point I wasn't sure whether they were comprehending what I was saying, so I picked up a bit of chalk and drew a roasted chicken in a tray on the blackboard.

'This is "roasted,"' I said slowly.

'Roasted,' they repeated obediently.

I drew another plucked chicken.

'This one is "raw."'

We started on verbs – walk, run, crawl. The kids were hanging on my every word. If I wasn't sure if they understood what I was saying, I acted it out like a game of charades. When I jumped up and down and said, 'Jump, jump, jump,' some of them were laughing too hard to repeat it.

Before I knew it, the hour was up. Their exuberance was so infectious that I had temporarily forgotten I had a hangover. With a sense of the surreal, I dismissed my first class.

'Well done,' said Saki afterwards. 'Especially considering it was your first class and you had no time to prepare.'

I wished Saki well for her lesson and then headed past the dozens of bicycles that were lined up out the front of the school. I was on a high. I'd done something tangible to help. My students' eagerness to learn was beautiful, but also heartbreaking. I hoped they got the chance to use English and make a good living, but I also hoped that one day there would be more opportunities for them to do well-paid and meaningful work in their own language.

I was scanning the oncoming traffic for a motorbike tuktuk when I spotted a big canvas sign on a gate across the road: 'BLOOD DONATIONS URGENTLY NEEDED'. In the corner was the UN emblem.

I went inside and met a lovely young nurse called Chantrea who explained that a dengue fever outbreak had caused a blood shortage in the province. She grew excited when I told her that my blood type is O-Negative, because it is the only blood type that can be used in an emergency situation when a patient's blood type is unknown, and it is also rare.

Chantrea asked me to lie down on a hospital bed as she prepared the syringe.

'You have beautiful veins,' she said admiringly. 'They are so easy to find.'

'Um, thanks,' I replied. It was surely the weirdest compliment I'd received.

When she was done, Chantrea took a photo of me giving a thumbs up from the hospital bed to send to Mum and Dad. We said goodbye and I skipped back outside. The day was turning out well: I had done two good things.

EVEN THOUGH I came prepared for my second English class, for some reason it was more challenging than the first. Maybe it was the mix of students or my Australian accent, but I wasn't sure whether they understood a word of what I said. When I kept getting blank looks, I reverted to the blackboard and started drawing pictures. That seemed to help, so I spent the rest of the lesson drawing on the board. I was sorry that they didn't have someone qualified for the job.

The following day I taught back-to-back classes for beginners and advanced students. At the end of the second class, a boy asked me if I could spare another thirty minutes to give him a one-on-one lesson. He attended classes three times a week because he wanted to learn English quickly. He was desperate to escape from his job as a laundry boy, where he worked twelve hours a day, seven days a week. His boss gave him time off to come to lessons, but that was his only free time. I gave him another lesson on the porch outside the classroom. He seemed very bright and thanked me with a beautiful smile.

I treated myself with a massage in the afternoon at Seeing Hands, which is staffed by blind masseuses. A man dressed in blue scrubs emerged from behind a curtain. I was shocked by the sight of his empty eye sockets. He smiled and quietly asked me to follow him to a massage table halfway down the room. I guess he must have memorised the layout of the furniture. I lay face down on the table and closed my eyes. Perhaps his sense of touch was heightened due to him lacking vision because it was an incredible massage.

The route back to the guesthouse took me past a collection of shanties that jutted out over a brown river choked with garbage. Some of the shacks only had three walls, so I could see through to the single room where entire families slept, cooked, ate, reproduced and played. A little girl peered out of a shack that was made from bits of cardboard. I guiltily thought about the family home that was waiting for me back in Melbourne. It had a pool and a tennis court and a bedroom just for me.

I was glad to have taught a few English classes, but I knew I was deluded if I thought my contribution would actually fix anything. It was like trying to plug a leak in the *Titanic* with a roll of sticky tape. It also wasn't a shortcut to not feeling guilty about my wealth and privilege. This was something I'd need to get used to somehow.

When I got back to the guesthouse, I booked a seat on a boat travelling to Battambang the following morning. I felt bad not to be staying on longer; those poor kids must have teachers stopping and starting all the time. But I had come to Cambodia to see Cambodia, so I couldn't stay on indefinitely.

So much had happened in the past couple of weeks that I wanted to send my first group email before I moved on. I retrieved my handheld computing device and collapsible keyboard from my backpack and set myself up at the table and chair in my room. I'd splurged on the device, known as a PDA, before I'd left. It was far cheaper than a laptop, and it was a lot lighter too, and it made it possible to draft emails at my leisure rather than paying for heaps of hours at internet cafes. I also used it to write a few children's stories each month for a small start-up magazine called *Students' Journey*. I'd started writing for them before leaving home as a way of earning extra cash.

It took me almost an hour to set out my thoughts. I began by saying how my life seemed to have turned technicolour: every individual moment was interesting, if not completely fascinating. I described the horrors of the genocide museum, eating 'weird' food in Phnom Penh and getting sick on duck fetus (minus the most embarrassing details), and the fun of exploring Angkor Wat's extraordinary temples with Dario and Justin. Before signing off, I said how incredible it was to suddenly feel like a millionaire in Cambodia, but I'd realised it was only because its people were so poor. Cambodia was delightfully different from Australia, but I was having a hard time processing the poverty.

There are rats in the rubbish, children in the gutters, amputees galore, and the whole economy is dependent on tourism. Only members of the corrupt government can get ahead in life, I've been told.

The people must also have a lot of trauma to cope with from the war, but I've noticed that they smile a lot. Or maybe they smile when they see me because I am a possible transaction? I've heard other backpackers say about the Cambodians, 'Oh they are poor, but they are such a happy people.' It annoys me when people say that, because then they can argue with a tuktuk driver over thirty cents and feel wounded when they aren't the victor barterer.

So yes, while it's great for travellers to do everything dirt cheap, unless you're blinkered (and some people I've met here are), it's also very sad.

Anyway, maybe I am not making any sense. I dunno, but I'll keep you posted on The World According to Jeska, don't you worry. (Worry!)

ONCE AT AN INTERNET CAFÉ, I opened the folder containing the email addresses of about thirty of my friends and family members. I added Dario and Matthew's names to the list, then I read over the email one last time and hit send.

I spent the rest of the afternoon wondering whether Matthew would reply. It was the first direct contact we'd had in over six months. Perhaps he would just write a couple of lines to wish me well on my big trip. He knew that I'd been excited about it.

Oh, come on. Who was I kidding? There was no chance Matthew would reply. Not after what I'd done the last time I'd attempted to make contact with him.

It was so cringeworthy I'd been trying to block out the memory ever since. And yet the events of that night were still painfully vivid. I'd gone to my friend Paul's housewarming party in North Melbourne, which happened to be just around the corner from Matthew's place, where I had spent so many weekends during the months we were together. We'd already broken up twice by then, but I had a lot to drink at the party and in my drunken state I got it into my head that I should go see Matthew.

Without telling anyone or even thinking it through, I snuck away from the party and practically jogged to Matthew's modern apartment complex. When I reached the intercom at the front gate, I decided not to ask Matthew to buzz me in. That would just be like talking to him on the phone, and that had never gotten us anywhere. I needed to speak to him in person.

I went around to the side fence and tried to scale it, but it was too high. So I went back to the entrance and checked the coast was clear, then lay down on the driveway and slid underneath the gate. I almost got stuck and had to suck in my breath to fit through.

I went up the fire escape stairs and came out at the second floor. Just to be back in the familiar place with its patterned carpet and pleasant new building smell made my heart thump. To see him would take my breath away. I knocked on the door with a shaking hand.

Unfortunately, it wasn't Matthew who answered, but his flatmate, Swanny. She was also an ABC producer and I'd always felt uncomfortable around her. She was about twenty years older than me, but that wasn't the reason. Even though she was pleasant enough, I'd always had the feeling she didn't like me.

Swanny was in her pyjamas and looked understandably surprised to see me at the door. I didn't offer an explanation as to how I got in the building.

'Is Matthew home?' I asked.

'No, he's at the pub,' she said.

'Will he be home soon?'

'I have no idea.' She looked at me with a touch of disdain.

I started to cry.

'Do you want to come in?'

I could tell she didn't mean it.

'It's okay,' I said. 'I'll send him a text message.'

'Okay. Bye, Jess.'

The door closed and I slunk away into the darkness. As I went back down the stairs, I sent Matthew a garbled message about having 'popped in' and signed off by saying that I was going back to Paul's party – as though that were cool.

I woke up stone-cold sober the next morning. As the events of the night before came flooding back, my stomach filled with lead. I had crossed the line into criminality by trespassing onto an ex-boyfriend's property.

No email could ever bring me back from that.

SUFFICE TO SAY that when I checked my inbox the following day, there was no email from Matthew. But there was one from Mum, who was hyperventilating about the photo of me lying on the hospital bed after giving blood.

'Jessica Mary! You could have got a blood disease!' she wrote.

Mum used to be a nurse so I was surprised by her alarm – I thought she'd be proud. I sent a reply reassuring her that the nurse was very professional and that the clinic was funded by the United Nations, so international standards of hygiene were surely practised.

'It was a good way to help people here,' I added.

I smiled as I read an email from Dario. His command of written English was shaky, but what he wrote was very sweet. He said he thought of me often, and that his cavities were fixed and it hadn't cost very much. He was moving on to the beaches of southern Thailand in the morning and would be in Malaysia within a week or two.

Dario was sweet and superhot and he liked me. Maybe I should stop thinking of myself as the version I was around Matthew. It wasn't the person that Dario saw, and it wasn't who I really was.

Next I read a reply to my group email from Lisa, who was a friend from law school. She was busy at work so she had to be quick, but she told me how she had kissed a guy at a nightclub just after I left. Something about the kiss made her fall in love with him, but they hadn't swapped numbers. So she went back to the club the following weekend and got his number from his friends. Her hopes were pinned on hooking up with him again. The places she mentioned seemed familiar and alien at the same time.

I recoiled a little when I read her last line.

MISS YA BABE. *Have fun – and remember you're there for the cultural experience and to contribute what you can – no one expects you to save the world.*

'SAVE THE WORLD?' Oh no. Had I come off like some kind of do-gooder gallivanting around Cambodia? It hadn't been my intention. But how could anyone see the poverty and do nothing? Wasn't I just responding the way all newcomers did?

When my defensiveness eventually wore off, I had to admit that I actually did want to save the world – even if I could only help a tiny part of it. But I had no idea how.

7

ISLAND LIFE

I handed the boatman three tatty American dollar bills. He nodded his thanks before flicking his cigarette butt into the river and stuffing the notes into his money belt. He took my pack and then offered me his hand as I stepped onto the boat, which wobbled beneath us in the shallows. I sat on a plank of wood in front of him and put my feet up on my pack. He revved the longboat's motor and we began to chug along the calm waters of the Tonle Sap. The river was so wide that I couldn't make out much of the riverbank opposite, other than dense mangroves and a few swaying palms. All the same, it was exciting to get my first glimpse of Laos.

Voen Khan border had opened to foreigners six years earlier, making it Cambodia's second land border (the first was with Thailand). I'd read and reread the steps laid out in my guidebook for crossing the border, which included getting an exit permit from the seedy border town of Stung Treng the day before. I just hoped I hadn't missed out anything, because I was kind of in the middle of nowhere. According to my guidebook, 'Cambodia and Laos share a remote frontier that includes some of the wildest areas of both countries.' I hadn't seen another backpacker since the day before when I was checking into the guesthouse, and the island of Don Det where I was headed had no electricity. While in Cambodia I'd travelled to the fairly remote regions of Mondulkiri and Ratanakiri, but this was apparently further flung. To make my money last for a full year, I needed to avoid buying flights, so an overland route was my best option.

However, I started to question my choices when I arrived at the border checkpoint on the east side of the riverbank about thirty minutes later. A young immigration policeman holding an enormous assault rifle frowned at me from behind a desk as I entered the small wooden building. Guns made me jumpy and it looked as if he was having a bad day. It's not like anyone would know if he dispatched me.

With a thumping heart and a watery smile, I walked over to him.

'Passport,' he said.

I silently passed it over. He flicked straight to the page containing my visa, which I'd arranged from the Laotian embassy back in Phnom Penh. It was a full-page reflective sticker featuring a complex design in shades of purple, pink and blue, which was presumably hard to counterfeit. It was printed in English, French and the intricate Laotian script.

'Photocopies.'

I gave him a photocopy of my passport and visa.

'Exit permit.'

At this point, a second guard wandered in and muttered something to the first policeman as he sat down next to him. He too was armed to the teeth.

'ID photos,' said the first policeman, just as brusque as before.

I retrieved two passport-sized photos from the stash I kept in the plastic pocket of my passport holder. The policeman looked at the photo, then at me, and then back at the photo.

'You are pretty,' he said. It sounded more like a command than a compliment, but there was a small smile on his lips.

'Thank you,' I replied. I wasn't exactly going to play at modesty by disagreeing with him.

Having furnished the policeman with all the required documents, he began recording my visa details in a massive ledger. He stamped the day's date across the passport page in red: 1 July 2006. Then he stamped another part of the same page with some kind of seal and scrawled his signature over the top. He gave me back my passport. My thirty days in Laos had begun.

However, the day's travels were not yet over. Out the front of the building was a minibus, which waited another twenty minutes before it took me and a few locals, plus three hessian bags of rice and a couple of live chickens along a dirt road for about half an hour. For reasons that were unclear to me, when we reached a village I was instructed to get out, and I did the next part of the journey on the back of a motorbike. I concentrated hard at keeping my balance on the back with my pack on, because I knew that if I leaned too far to one side I'd topple off. The motorbike driver dropped me off at a dock where a few boats must have spent most of their days waiting for passengers.

One of the three men quoted me five dollars to take me to Don Det in the riverine archipelago of Si Phan Don, which translates to 'four thousand islands'. It was a big sum for a short trip, but there was a lack of alternatives and I was effectively chartering the whole longboat. Anyhow, the scenery alone was worth five dollars. We glided through the copper-coloured river in magnificent afternoon light, with streaks of orange and a lick of pink across the sky. The longboat took gentle detours around the mangroves sprouting up out of the water, where the current formed foam-lipped eddies.

Enormous, umbrella-shaped rain trees grew along the fertile banks. As Don Det came into view, I saw thatched bamboo shacks on stilts lining its edge, with the occasional longboat tethered underneath.

I had no idea what life was like for the people who lived inside the shacks. In fact, I could virtually count on one hand all the things I knew about their country. The introductory chapters in my guidebook had informed me that Laos was a one-party communist state that was landlocked and mountainous, and had one of the highest poverty rates in Southeast Asia. The majority religion in the former French colony was Buddhism. With just about every other country in the world, I had at least some kind of superficial association to describe it. Italy? Pizza. Spain? Bullfights. Norway? Reindeer. India? My favourite cuisine. But I didn't associate anything with Laos. I didn't know of any famous Laotians, and the only person I knew who had been there had just told me that it was pretty and the people were kind. I'd looked for books on Laos at a few bookstores in Cambodia, but I hadn't been able to find any. As my guidebook said, 'This is one of the last quiet countries on earth.' Laos just didn't really project an image to the outside world.

I was excited to find out everything I could, but I would begin the following day. By the time I took off my backpack in my one-dollar-per-night bungalow, it was dusk. With no electricity and only one tiny window, my room was almost completely dark. It had been a long day and I was tired. The day had begun with the two-hour boat ride at 7 am from Stung Treng and was followed by lots of waiting around and innumerable modes of transport. I lay on the bed to rest before dinner and the next thing I knew it was morning.

I awoke to the sounds of male voices speaking in German. I wriggled out from under the mosquito net, put on a fresh t-shirt and fisherman pants and went outside to say hello. Two guys lay facing each other on a hammock on the balcony of the bungalow next to mine. A third sat on the steps. He was dressed in black and wore eyeliner, and he told me that they were talking about how profoundly different people were in East and West Germany, despite the fall of the Berlin Wall almost twenty years ago. I was starving and they seemed kind of intense and unhappy, so I didn't linger long before heading to the restaurant at the jetty for some breakfast.

That was when I first caught sight of Joe. He appeared to be having an argument with a water buffalo. It was thrashing around in the shallows and straining against the rope around its neck, which had Joe on one end and a young local guy on another. Both were lithe and quick on their feet, but they were no match for the water buffalo, which must have weighed at least four hundred kilograms. Three other guys joined in the battle of wills and brute strength, while a couple of street dogs watched on with cocked ears, ready to nip if called upon. There were cheers when the poor creature finally succumbed to being loaded onto a barge, where one water buffalo had stood quietly amidst the commotion.

Joe put his t-shirt back on and came in for breakfast. He took a seat at the table next to mine.

'Well done,' I said, in between sips of my second black coffee. 'That looked like hard work.'

'It certainly was,' he said with a delightful Irish accent. 'Now I know where the saying "Stubborn as an ox" comes from.' He laughed. 'I think I've earned myself a decent breakfast.'

We introduced ourselves and as Joe tucked into a massive omelette, he told me that a farmer downstream had leased the water buffalos to plough his rice paddies. I was relieved to hear they weren't off to market. We kept chatting and a few other travellers wandered in. When everyone had a full belly, we headed off on hired bicycles to explore the island.

I SLOWED DOWN and got in sync with island life. I walked or rode a bicycle everywhere and spent a couple of afternoons reading my book in the hammock. Sending emails was out. Don Det had only one computer, which was solar-powered and connected to the internet via a Nokia mobile phone. It was crazy expensive, with users charged by the minute. I sent a quick email to Mum and Dad saying that I had crossed the border without any issues, and that was it.

Don Det was also perfectly set up for making friends. A generator provided four hours of electricity at the main restaurant in the evening, so backpackers tended to congregate there for dinner and beers. After my first full day on the island, I found myself sharing a table with eight Europeans, including Irish Joe and a really nice Scottish guy called Tom, who had longish curly red hair and glasses. There were four girls and five guys, and among us was just one couple, who were British and almost unbelievably good-looking. We ate plates of noodles and swapped travel stories – the good, the bad and the embarrassing. I was having the best time. Yes, I was drunk – we all were – but everyone seemed fascinating and the conversation felt very honest. After all, what was the point of being reserved? We would only know one another for a brief moment in time. We had only just met and we came from different countries, yet these people kind of felt like old friends. Maybe it was because we shared a core belief: that the world was worthy of exploring.

As the table filled with empty bottles of Beer Laos and overflowing ashtrays, we started discussing world politics and collectively lamented the war in Iraq led by American president George Bush.

'I have a radical idea,' I said. By this time I was drunk enough to believe that what I was about to say may actually be profound. 'Governments should fund a year of international travel for every young person after they finish school. I've only been away for a month, but I feel like I've already learned a lot of things I was never taught at school. If people could experience foreign cultures, they would realise how similar we are as humans and would know better than to hold racist or bigoted beliefs. It could put an end to wars.'

'Do you think governments would ever agree to pay for it though?' asked Tom, as he topped up my mug of beer.

'Well, it would be cheaper than fighting endless wars.'

'Yeah, maybe.'

Just then the waitress came over with a tray of shot glasses filled with a clear alcohol.

'Jess, get ready: this is Lao-Lao rice whisky,' said Tom, who had been in the country for a few days already.

'It costs less than a dollar a litre and it's about seventy per cent alcohol,' added Matt, who was from Devon in the UK. 'It will knock your head off.'

'Cheers everyone,' said Joe with a mischievous wink.

'Cheers!'

Spluttering, I said, 'That's unbelievably potent stuff.'

The hot liquorice sensation was still burning the back of my throat when Joe waved the waitress back over to order us another round of shots.

'Again?' I asked incredulously.

'We've got to maintain the pace,' Joe replied with mock seriousness, as though he were talking about administering first aid.

'If crazy Irishman Joe says that we need another shot, then we need another,' said Tom.

I laughed. 'Okay.'

By the time the restaurant was plunged into darkness at 11 pm, I'd lost track of how many shots we'd had. We settled our bill and then stumbled back to our bungalows by torchlight. We had to stop for a bit because Tom did a wee in the bushes and Joe and Matt were doubled over with laughter. As I waited for their chuckles to subside, I gazed up at the half moon and its milky reflection in the Mekong. The millions of stars overhead were incredible.

THE FOLLOWING AFTERNOON, a group of local guys asked my friends and I if we fancied a game of soccer. Even though I was a bit out of shape, I was up for it. I loved soccer (which I was learning to call 'football') and had been also missing my weekly hockey matches in Melbourne.

However, we realised it was more than a friendly kick when our opponents reappeared in red jerseys and told us that two of them were national players. They had in fact just returned from a regional tournament where they represented Laos. Spectators emerged in the form of half a dozen monks. They sat on the steps of a nearby temple, where robes had been hung on the balcony to dry like bright-orange sheets. 'Team Euro' as Tom named us, were a scrappy bunch. We were almost broken by our hangovers and lacked proper footwear. We played in sandals or went barefoot, and with the exception of me – the only girl on the field – were bare-chested too.

At any rate, even the best soccer boots wouldn't have been much help, because the pint-sized pitch was as sodden as a rice paddy from the heavy rains earlier in the afternoon. Minutes after the game began, the ridiculously good-looking British boyfriend extended his leg to connect with the ball whizzing past, lost his balance and slid several metres on his backside. When he got back up, he was covered in mud. We were squelching around like mud wrestlers and laughing our heads off.

In less than five minutes, one of the national players scored the first goal, causing Joe, our goalie, to swear as only a plucky Irishman can. The goalscorer leaped up a nearby palm tree. He wrapped his arms and legs around the trunk and grinned down at us.

Tom passed to me and I crossed it to Matt, who scored.

'Nice work, Lady Jane,' shouted Joe.

This nickname stuck for the rest of the match, which cracked me up.

Meanwhile, the national players were lightning on their feet and the locals clearly played together as a team pretty often. As a consequence, one of the national players seemed to spend half his time up the tree celebrating yet another goal.

We'd been playing for about twenty minutes when Matt did a huge kick across the pitch that was meant to go to an Austrian guy, but instead collided with the statue of a mythical serpent on top of the steps of the monastery, shattering its head.

'Oh no,' said Matt. Looking stricken, he turned to the monks with his hands clasped. 'I am so, so sorry.'

'It's okay,' said one. 'No problem.'

The other monks smiled graciously and urged us to return to the game. Boy was I relieved that it hadn't been me.

Team Euro was outskilled and outpaced by Team Laos, who defeated us twenty-one to twelve in the exceptionally high-scoring match. Sweaty and slathered in mud, we shook hands with our opponents and congratulated them. Then we headed back to clean ourselves up with a cold shower before undertaking the nightly ritual of beers, deep and meaningful conversation, and copious shots of rice whisky.

8
LOST AND FOUND

I arrived in the capital city of Vientiane on the overnight bus from Pakse feeling grumpy and fatigued. I swore it was the first and last 'sleeper bus' I would take, because despite its name I hadn't slept a wink. Theoretically I should have been able to because my seat reclined to an almost flat position. However, the bus had groaned and shaken at every turn, and the journey had seemed a never-ending series of bends. The lights also stayed on all night and the atmosphere grew increasingly stinky as the body odours and food scraps of fifty sweaty backpackers commingled.

But the worst part of the experience was racist Dave. He was sitting on my left and I had made the mistake of being friendly towards him at the start of the journey when he told me he was Australian. After he plunged into a long treatise about why Asians are 'backward', I did my level best to give him the cold shoulder, but he didn't seem to take the hint. Dave trailed behind me like a whiny puppy at every food and toilet stop. He was one of those people who couldn't seem to be alone – maybe because he was rubbish company.

Dave wanted to share a room with me when we got to Vientiane, so when the journey finally ended sixteen hours later, I mumbled something about being sick and practically jogged to a guesthouse that I had surreptitiously looked up in my Lonely Planet.

I lost half of that first day in Vientiane catching up on sleep. When I emerged in the afternoon I was still a bit groggy, which was perhaps partly why I couldn't seem to find something as obvious as a monument known as the 'Arc de Triomphe of Vientiane'.

Navigating the streets as a pedestrian was difficult. Through the centre of the city there was an eight-lane road with a concrete divider running down the middle, so I walked for six blocks without being able to cross the road. I was frustrated by the lack of street signs and while poring over my map, I almost fell into an open sewer through a hole in the footpath. After a frustrating hour, I grumpily gave up on seeing the monument, at least for that day.

Instead I changed course and started heading towards the Lao National Museum, which was where the French governor lived until Laos gained its independence in 1953. I found myself in an industrial part of town that was interesting in a bleak sort of way, so I kept going despite knowing I was heading in the wrong direction. There were a handful of mechanics, tyre shops, brickyards and what appeared to be a string of factories. Unexpectedly in the mix was a women's clothing boutique. I went inside to try on the red cotton shrug that the mannequin in the window was wearing. I felt like an absolute giant next to the young shop assistant, who found me an 'extra large' and guided me into a corner of the shop that was partitioned with a black curtain and had a long mirror leaning up against the wall. I put the shrug on over my singlet and immediately decided to buy it – covered shoulders were more pleasing in a modest society like Laos, and it wouldn't make me too hot. I went over to the register and gave the shop assistant 10,000 kip.

'Khob chai,' I ventured uncertainly as she passed me my bag.

The girl's face lit up and she said something I didn't understand. I had a bad ear for languages, so I was happy that my first attempt at saying 'thank you' in Laotian was passable.

Back on the street, I looked at my watch and realised that it was too close to closing time at the museum to make a visit worthwhile. I decided to get a massage before dinner at the place I'd seen near my guesthouse. The long bus ride had aggravated the soreness in my lower back, which I attributed to carrying a backpack that was too heavy for me. When I'd started my trip it weighed fourteen kilos, but it was probably closer to twenty now. I was hopeless at travelling light. I kept seeing cool stuff that I couldn't just walk past (and oops, I'd just done it again). Books were my biggest weakness. It was just plain stupid to be carrying a collection of nine paperbacks (two were guidebooks, but even so). I told myself that I would read like mad for the next few days, or else be forced to make some difficult decisions about how to lighten my load.

I started heading towards the massage place and was almost there when I came upon a nondescript streetside café. Sitting at one of the tables was an overweight, red-faced Westerner with a prepubescent girl on his lap. He looked to be in his mid-fifties and he was sort of jigging the tiny girl on his knee. One hand gripped her waist as he laughed and chatted away with his Western buddy. There were empty coffee cups on the table and the two men looked as though they didn't have a care in the world. The little girl just sat there with a blank expression on her face, like a doll. Was it this easy to commit a heinous crime in broad daylight in Vientiane? My eyes flashed with anger, but the man was too absorbed in his odious world to notice me. I gave him daggers anyway and continued walking.

At the massage place a young woman motioned for me to follow her upstairs. At the top was a sort of attic that was divided into segments for customers, although the timber partitions were only hip height. A strip of faded red carpet ran through the middle of the room. She led me into the first massage cubicle on the left and I lay down, fully clothed, on a mattress on the floor. I pointed to where the soreness was and she began to tread all over my back. She was as light as a feather, and it felt amazing.

At first I was only half aware of a man's muffled voice nearby. I couldn't make out what he was saying, but I detected an unmistakable tone of urgency and aggression. Either his masseuse said nothing or her reply was so quiet as to be inaudible. The next couple of minutes passed in silence. Then I heard a faint groan. My own masseuse continued to wordlessly knead my back. The male voice, then cheerful, thanked his masseuse and two sets of footsteps went down the stairs. All I could hear was the sound of my breath rising and falling. My skin was crawling and I couldn't wait to get out of there.

I was struck by the fact that sex work seemed to be the consequence for countless young women living in poverty. It made me angry, but mostly sad. I returned to the guesthouse and tried to escape into one of my books.

I WAS STILL FEELING a bit flat the following morning as I ate a crusty baguette with egg and mayo for breakfast at a no-frills café. Vientiane was the first place on my travels that I hadn't really warmed to. Even aside from the disturbing visibility of pedophilia and sex work, there was something that struck me as a bit depressing. Other than the dull roar of traffic, Vientiane felt like a sleepy city, though in a suppressed way rather than a relaxed one. The city's buildings were mostly drab and boxy –

unlike Phnom Penh, there wasn't much remaining French architecture and it lacked the Cambodian capital's colour and vitality. The baguettes were decidedly delicious though. I'd just taken my final bite when the doors swung open and in walked Tom. I leaped out of my seat.

'Tom!'

'Jess!'

We hugged.

'How funny to bump into you,' Tom said in his endearing Scottish accent. 'How are you doing?'

'I'm okay, but so far I'm not really loving Vientiane.' I was too embarrassed to mention the massage place, but I told him about the crappy overnight bus ride and not being able to find what I was looking for. Soon enough, Tom had me laughing again. We agreed to meet up for drinks that night, along with Matt from Devon, who had taken the bus from Pakse with Tom a couple of days earlier.

After that first bit of good luck, everything started going right again. I headed off to the post office to send a long letter to my grandmother and on my way I practically tripped over the Arc de Triomphe of Vientiane. It was a mystery as to how I'd managed to miss it as it was huge and immediately recognisable. It seemed strange to replicate the famous French monument as a way of commemorating those Laotians who had died in the 1949 independence war against the French colonial regime.

I paid the eight hundred kip admission fee, which was the equivalent of just ten American cents, and began walking up the first of several flights of stairs. I avoided the souvenir displays on every level. The items being sold mostly consisted of t-shirts featuring the monument. There must have been thousands of the same design in different colours.

According to my guidebook, the monument had been built between 1957 and 1968 using cement the United States had donated on the proviso that it would be used to build an airport runway. When the communist party overthrew the Royal Laotian Government in 1975 and ended a six-hundred-year-old monarchy, the monument was renamed from 'Anousavali', which simply means 'Monument' to 'Patuxai', which translates to 'Victory Gate'. Apparently Patuxai still wasn't finished, though to me it looked ready for some maintenance, as the concrete was marked with patches of black grime from decades of monsoon rains. From the top the view of the flat-as-a-pancake terrain was unremarkable, so I only stayed up there a few minutes.

That night I met up with Tom and Matt at Small Bar, which had pool tables and a cheerful yellow decor. They introduced me to Veira from Slovakia and Victoria from Germany, who were staying at the same guesthouse as them. The girls were funny and interesting and they invited me to join them the following day on a trip to the quirky sculpture complex called Buddha Park and a traditional herbal spa and sauna. I was excited – a girls' day would be a real treat.

Irish Joe busted in at around 10 pm and gave me a bear hug, then picked me up and spun me around. Next he ordered us all a double round of shots. Tom and I began a game of pool and he cleared the floor with me. I took revenge by shaking the talcum powder over him that was meant to be used as hand chalk. He returned the favour until we both looked like drunk ghosts. As the six of us made our way home around midnight on the deserted, unlit streets, we watched for open sewers. Apparently a backpacker had fallen in one a few days before.

A COUPLE OF DAYS LATER, I said goodbye to Tom once again. He was off to Phonsavan in the morning and was slowly heading northwards to China. My next stop was the riverside town of Vang Vieng, where I planned on teaching English for a week at a language school Victoria had told me about.

'Thanks for making Vientiane so fun,' I said to Tom after we'd hugged goodbye. 'I'm so glad I bumped into you here.'

'See you, Jess. Enjoy your travels.'

'You too.'

I went back to my family-run guesthouse, as the mother and her two sons had invited me to prepare alms for the monks. We sat around a table in the foyer folding 10,000-kip notes while snacking on sticky rice and drinking beer – except for the mum, who sipped green tea from a tiny porcelain cup. A fluffy white terrier sat obediently next to her on a chair. His little head was cocked in interest at her work. Her eldest son, Khamla, invited me to go to a nearby monastery where some of his friends were monks. I eagerly agreed and we headed off on the back of his motorbike.

It was a peaceful monastery, with lots of trees in the compound and neatly swept paths. As we entered the dormitory, half a dozen monks turned to look at us in mild surprise. They were sitting cross-legged on a floral carpet on the floor, smoking cigarettes and watching television. My eyes widened at the posters of busty women in bikinis on the walls. There were another couple of guys in football jerseys, who I figured were also lay people like me. It almost appeared to be a monk frat-house party.

We took a seat on the carpet and had some green tea as Khamla told the monks that I was a backpacker from Australia who was travelling the world. I retrieved my PDA device from my bag, as a show-and-tell depended less on a shared language. One of the monks clearly had an eye for technology, as he spent almost an hour fiddling with it. Using the small touch-pen, he drew a picture of me on the screen.

'It is you,' he said as he held it up to show me.

I smiled and thanked him, and another monk grinned and gave him the thumbs up.

'I will write you a letter,' he said.

When he handed the device back to me to read, I tried not to burst out laughing. I'd been expecting some serene words of Buddhist wisdom, but he was flirting with me. The monk had written: 'You are a pretty lady from Australia. I like your hair. You stay in Laos a long time.'

At dawn the next day I joined Khamla and his family in giving alms. Eleven monks approached the guesthouse and lined up out the front in single file. They were carrying silver alms bowls and their orange robes were draped across both shoulders. Khamla's mum bowed solemnly with her hands clasped together in the prayer position. Then she spooned some sticky rice into their alms bowls. Khamla smiled and nodded at me to indicate it was my turn. I tried to keep a neutral expression on my face as I walked over to them with the huge bowl of kip, but I was so excited to be giving alms to monks. However, my original deference had dropped a notch and was probably at a more realistic level. I had learned that some monks are just regular guys in robes.

9

THE BANANA PANCAKE TRAIL

I hadn't enjoyed anything about the bus journey that brought me to Vientiane, but the one leaving it was a delight. The pink double-decker bus was comfy and luxuriously air-conditioned: judging from all the Chinese characters on its side, it was a gift from Lao's powerful neighbour. It was a fairly short journey of four hours and I was sitting next to a fellow Aussie called Dom who was thoughtful and funny. He was also very cute, with curly light brown hair, freckles, blue eyes and a short beard with a ginger tinge. He had studied social work at uni, which I took as a strong indication that he must have a lot of empathy. He was very encouraging when I said that I was going to teach English in Vang Vieng.

Dom told me all about his close-knit family in Adelaide. His father was a successful potter who often sold his creations to Australia's Department of Foreign Affairs, who gifted them to visiting dignitaries. Queen Elizabeth had even acquired some during her most recent visit to Australia.

'That's amazing,' I gushed. 'Your dad must be so talented. Are you artistic too?'

'Not really. I used to like drawing as a kid. My girlfriend is really into art though,' he said. 'So I'm surrounded by creative types.'

Damn it, I thought. *I've got a huge crush on someone who isn't available.*

To pass the time as the bus slowly wound its way through the scenic mountain roads, I brought out my headphone splitter so we could both listen to the same music. I played one of my favourite songs on my iPod, and then Dom played me one of his. We both liked indie and folk music, plus stuff from the sixties and seventies.

'Wow, that seemed quick,' I said as the bus pulled into Vang Vieng.

'It did. I guess we had lots to talk about,' said Dom with a smile that crinkled his eyes.

We began walking along the smooth dirt road towards the guesthouse that we'd chosen from the guidebook. Ahead of us lay stunning karst mountains, which were a mix of dense forest and rocky limestone outcrops. We chatted away happily as we passed a string of bars and restaurants, a post office and an internet café.

'Would you like to share a room?' I suddenly blurted out. I held my breath, expecting Dom to laugh at my audacity.

'Sure,' he said. 'It will be cheaper.'

'Exactly,' I replied.

Hooray.

We took a left down a little lane and checked into a guesthouse overlooking the Nam Song River, which ran parallel to the main street. After dumping our stuff in the room (which of course had two single beds), Dom and I headed straight back out for an early dinner and drinks.

'Xayoh Café looks good to me,' said Dom about an open-air bar and restaurant that was playing a Justin Timberlake track. A few dozen backpackers were milling about with drinks in their hands.

'Let's do it,' I said.

Within minutes we were chatting with others, and moved up the back to where there were comfy cushions on the floor with a low table. There was Matheo from France, Christian from Germany, Werner from South Africa, and his girlfriend, Rachel, who was from Texas. She was taller than me and had a porcelain-white complexion, with big brown eyes and dark hair in a soft pixie bob. Incredibly, Irish Joe was there too, talking to some other people before he came over to say hi. He was like the mist on the mountains: he vanished during the day and reappeared at night. Everyone seemed to know him, but I got the sense that nobody knew him properly.

I happily settled in for another evening of stimulating conversation. I loved hearing stories about the places the backpackers had been and the home countries they had left behind. I had a couple of tales now too.

Once again, everyone seemed fantastic. The only person I was a little unsure about was Rachel. She peppered her sentences with big words when small ones would do, referred to the Iraq War as a 'campaign' and defended George Bush's decision to invade it. She had just finished up teaching English in Taiwan and was about to find out whether she had gotten the diplomatic post she'd applied for. Deep down, I was envious of Rachel's easy confidence and direction in life. My lack of clarity was an agony.

After a couple of hours and many rounds of beers, we thought it would be funny to take photos of our feet, which had tiger stripe tan lines from wearing sandals day in and day out. We arranged our feet in a circle so that they looked like daisy petals, and then pointed our cameras downwards. I was looking back over my photos when I felt someone tap me on the shoulder.

'Tom!' I exclaimed. 'What are you doing here?'

'There wasn't all that much to see in Phonsavan so I thought I'd come here for a couple of days before going to Luang Prabang.'

Turning to the group, I said, 'Guys, this is Tom. We met on Don Det island, and then Vientiane, and now here. We've had the most incredible timing to keep bumping into each other.'

'Well, it's not that surprising,' said Rachel, taking a sip of her vodka and lime. 'The odds are pretty high of bumping into the same people on the Banana Pancake Trail.'

'The what?'

'The Banana Pancake Trail,' repeated Rachel. 'It's the well-worn backpacker path across Southeast Asia. It's the modern-day version of the Hippie Trail that used to exist in the sixties and seventies when it was popular to travel overland from Europe to Asia through Afghanistan and India. The restaurants and guesthouses along the Banana Pancake Trail have learned to cook foods that Westerners like, so you can eat banana pancakes just about anywhere.'

'Oh,' I said. 'I'd never heard of it. But why banana pancakes specifically?'

'Because bananas grow everywhere in Southeast Asia. It's sunny.'

'Oh I see. Well, there you go Tom – we were bound to meet again.'

I was disappointed to discover that I wasn't as intrepid as I'd thought I was. Without even knowing it, I'd been charting a predictable route.

Perhaps Tom sensed that I was a bit deflated because he turned to me and said, 'Why don't you meet up with me in China? You won't find any banana pancakes there.'

'Maybe I will, Tom,' I replied. 'Maybe I will.'

AFTER DISCOVERING that I was travelling along the Banana Pancake Trail, there suddenly seemed to be reminders of it everywhere – and not just on the menus, which I scoured with a new sense of irony. My peak banana-pancake moment came the following day when I spent an entire rainy afternoon eating pizza with the crew from Xayoh Café and watching reruns of *Friends* episodes at Friends Café, which showed the sitcom day and night, seven days a week.

Watching a familiar TV show felt like a guilty pleasure, but I also felt genuinely bad about not following through on my plan to teach English. I hadn't even gone to the language school to get more information. The idea had gone out the window because I didn't want to miss the chance to explore Vang Vieng with my fantastically fun friends. And, of course, that included gorgeous Dom, whose company I adored. Even though he gave no indication that he was going to make a move on me, I couldn't stop wishing that he would (and especially after he cheerily wished me goodnight and turned off the light in our room). I told myself that I would look for volunteering opportunities in other places, and that for the time being I should literally go with the flow down the Nam Song River.

The 'gang', as I referred to us in emails home, went on a series of outdoor excursions together. One morning we hired motorbikes and set out to explore the beautiful countryside. I thoroughly enjoyed it because I got to wrap my arms around Dom's waist as he navigated the precariously muddy rural roads. We passed villagers tending iridescent-green rice paddies and jumped into a stream where some kids were splashing around. At one point a naked toddler ran past us along a pinkish dirt track, carrying a bucket and shrieking with delight. It was so picturesque.

We found a local guide at the entrance of a karst limestone river cave. He gave us headlamps and we each hopped into an inflatable ring. We pulled ourselves through the cave using a fixed rope. It was pitch-black and the only sound was the drops of condensation plopping into the water below. At one point, the waters had risen so much from the rains that there was only a small gap between the ceiling and our inflatable rings. I talked myself out of succumbing to claustrophobia. To my relief, we soon came out into a cavernous space, but were then met with the incredible shrieking of bats. Even with headlamps it was too dark to make out their silhouette, but I could feel the wind from their beating wings as they flew overhead.

We were back in the beautiful bright sunshine and returning our headlamps when Christian said, 'You know, guys, I was just thinking that those bats might have had rabies. And the water in the cave would be filled with their droppings. I haven't been vaccinated against rabies. Do you think I should go to a clinic?'

'Technically it is possible to get rabies from bat poo – but it's highly unlikely,' said Rachel confidently. 'There were two cases of aerosol transmission in caves near my home town in Texas in the 1950s, but that was a one-off and apparently something about the caves was very unusual – I can't remember what though. But I'm quite certain you'd have to actually be bitten by a bat to get rabies.'

'Okay, phew,' said Christian.

'Speaking of vaccinations,' I said. 'Because I'm going to India, I had to get so many before I left that I made up a rap about them. I had eight injections – four in each arm. Twice.'

'How does the rap go?' asked Dom as we began walking back to our motorbikes.

'Well, it's pretty short,' I said. 'And I made up the bit about scabies because there isn't actually a vaccine for it. But scabies rhymes with rabies so—'

'Just sing it for us, Jess,' he urged me.

'All right. Here goes –

Black fever

Yellow fever

Rabies

Scabies

Polio

JAPANESE ENCYPHYLITIS.'

'Haha. You're such a weirdo, Jess,' said Dom. 'I love it.'

And I love you.

With a quiet sigh of longing, I hopped behind Dom on the motorbike and we sped off.

∼

THE NEXT DAY we went tubing, which is what had put Vang Vieng squarely on the backpacker map. It involved floating three kilometres down the Nam Song on the inner tube of a tractor tyre, like we'd used in the cave. The six of us got started just before lunch, and we'd only been drifting down the river for about ten minutes when a young Laos woman in a black halterneck dress beckoned for us to stop at her bar, which was a bamboo shack where thumping dance music was playing.

'Hey there! Free shots for everyone! Come and have a drink at Tropicana Bar,' she said in a sing-song voice. Next to her was a sign advertising 'welcome shots' and tequila buckets for two bucks.

We had a couple of rounds of drinks and some spring rolls and then hopped back in our tubes. We'd been in the water for an even shorter time when another woman persuaded us to stop at her bar.

'I get it now – tubing is a water-based bar crawl,' Tom said, chuckling, as we once again stacked our tubes on a wooden platform.

The third bar we stopped at was in a particularly pretty spot, with a thick canopy of lush rainforest enveloping the back of the tiny structure. There were bamboo mats laid out in a small section that served as a dance floor, and we started to dance next to another group of travellers, who from the looks of it had been drinking longer than we had. One of my favourite songs came on.

'Yes!' I shouted with delight, and started busting out my favourite moves.

I looked around at my friends dancing on the edge of the riverbank in their board shorts and bikinis with the stunning jungle backdrop behind them. Dom took another swig of beer and grinned at me as the next track began to play.

This is one of the coolest moments of my life.

The next bar had a rope swing at the end of a timber platform that was a few metres above the river. I was too content in my drunken haze to land with a slap into the waters below, but Werner and Christian had a go. Joe went next. He bellowed like Tarzan as he swung out over the river, then did a half flip and landed with a loud belly flop. We laughed.

'Ouch,' said Rachel. 'That must have hurt. Joe is nuts.'

'He cracks me up,' I said. 'He is a classic party boy.'

We continued on our way, this time with a bucket of pina colada and a straw as a takeaway. I gazed up at the sky and the dramatic outline of the mountains in the distance. Getting wasted in nature was trippy. We held hands to keep our tubes together in a massive circle as we drifted slowly down the river. Tom started singing the Bob Marley song that had been playing at the previous bar. We all joined in.

We stopped at a couple more bars. I'd lost count of how

many we'd been to. The leaves of the trees were dappled with late-afternoon sunlight when we came to a part of the river where there were a few parked minibuses waiting to shuttle drunk tubers back into town.

'Hey, guys – where's Joe?' I suddenly asked.

'Wasn't he with us at the last bar?' said Tom.

'Nah, he wasn't,' said Dom. 'My bet is that he's still doing shots somewhere further back along the river. Let's tell the minibus driver to keep an eye out for a drunk Irish guy.'

'That doesn't narrow it down much,' quipped Tom.

We went to our usual place for dinner, which was a popular choice because it was right next to where the bus was dropping off tubers. I'd hardly eaten anything all day and was absolutely starving. I tucked into a massive bowl of noodles. I nursed a beer, but couldn't finish it; I was done drinking for the day. Night fell and the last tubers had stumbled through the bar's doors some time ago, but Joe hadn't been among them.

'I'm a bit worried about Joe,' I said to Rachel. 'He was super wasted.'

'Me too. Last year a backpacker jumped off a rope swing and hit the rocks and broke his neck. He died.'

'Oh my god,' I said.

'Yeah. I don't want to worry you though. Joe is probably fine,' she added in a falsely bright tone. 'He's probably just partying with some new friends.'

We agreed to stay another hour. I was beginning to fear the worst when Joe suddenly walked through the door, his t-shirt speckled with vomit. He was incapable of stringing a sentence together and didn't seem to recognise us. He sat down, lit a cigarette and passed out in a chair. Rachel took the cigarette that was dangling from his hand and put it out. We exchanged relieved smiles and went to bed.

Our bump-ins were no longer accidental: the gang travelled to Luang Prabang as a group. We took up the back section of the bus, and laughed our heads off most of the way. Dom and I played the music game again.

As soon as I stepped off the bus, I fell head over heels for Luang Prabang. Draped in mist and nestled among verdant mountains, the World Heritage-listed city has well-preserved Buddhist monasteries and French architecture.

The next few days were bliss. We sipped fantastic coffee inside atmospheric French cafes as we watched the world go by, which included monks walking in their orange robes along the cobbled streets. Locals cruised by on scooters or in vintage French automobiles. We browsed beautiful bookstores and went to a film night at one of them. We swam at a series of stunning waterfalls. Luang Prabang was a heavenly blend of East and West.

We went to Full Moon Café every night for happy-hour gin and tonics and delectable pasta dishes. I could tell from the way some people were dressed that they were expats rather than backpackers. They were stylish and less hippy-looking than us. To me, they looked like the epitome of cool.

Dom kept me in a state of frustrated longing. He and I sometimes splintered off from the group to do things together, like exploring an incredible temple or enjoying a dinner at an Indian restaurant, because we both loved curries. We were still sharing a room. It was as if we were together, but we weren't.

During a rare period of alone time, I went to the Royal Palace Museum. It was a commanding white building with a mahogany roof and a sweeping driveway that was lined with palm trees and neat low hedges. Its many rooms had soaring ceilings and were filled with ornate gilt furniture. There were swords, screens and Buddha statues on display. One room was filled with gifts from foreign dignitaries, which I perused with interest. Australia had donated a boomerang made of unfinished wood that was strangely tattered; it looked as if some kids had played with it first. It seemed underwhelming beside the beautiful Japanese urns and delicately engraved ivory jewellery boxes from India.

Most impressive was the gift from the United States. Inside a display unit was a small Laotian flag and an engraved message from President Nixon above it that said: 'We went to the moon and carried your flag. We brought you back some pieces of the moon's surface.' And there inside the display case were three small black rocks. I couldn't believe I was staring at actual pieces of the moon.

There was no doubt that America could be a powerful friend or foe. Before it was lavishing gifts on Laos from outer space, it was dropping a torrent of bombs on the country. In 1964, the United States started bombing Laos every eight minutes, and it kept this up for nine whole years. More bombs were dropped on the small nation than were dropped in total during World War Two. Laos became the most bombed country per capita in history and a tenth of its population were killed. Tom had told me he had seen houses in Phonsavan that were made entirely out of old bomb casings.

Why inflict such misery on quiet Laos? It was due to America's hatred of communism. Lao's new communist government (which had deposed the royal family) had taken the side of the Vietnamese communists during the Vietnam War. The US had signed a UN peace agreement that prevented it from attacking Laos as a neutral state, so it took a sneaky, backdoor route: the bombing was carried out covertly by the Central Intelligence Agency (CIA) rather than government troops. Thus it was known as 'The Secret War'.

I was ruminating on how awful it all was as I walked back to the guesthouse. My thoughts were interrupted when I saw a 'For Rent' sign out the front of a lovely little house with a garden. I stopped and stared at the sign, which included the name of the real estate agent and a phone number.

What if I never went home to Australia? I could swap my boring nine-to-five existence with a charmed life in paradise. Luang Prabang had everything I needed: bookstores, film nights, spaghetti, gin and tonics, beautiful Buddhist temples and a tropical climate. I would never be bored for a single second. I would never be cold in winter and I would never have a depressing commute through rush hour to a dull job where I made countless spreadsheets and endlessly walked across the same bit of carpet.

Could I really do it, though? I'd have to learn Laotian. I had learned to count to ten and could even manage some basic transactions, but the idea of learning the whole language was overwhelming. I'd been hopeless at Mandarin in high school. And what would I do for work? If only I was qualified in something like health, which needs practitioners everywhere.

It's impossible. Forget it.

With a sigh, I continued walking up the hill. I had a quick shower and headed to the bowls club to meet up with the gang. Our fun for that evening was playing pétanque, a French sport that involved throwing hollow metal balls as close as possible to a small wooden ball on a gravel surface. Dom and I played as a team and we fluked a win.

I savoured every moment of the evening because it was my last night with my friends. I was getting the bus to Phonsavan the next morning before heading back to Vientiane. We were all travelling in different directions. Tom was off to China, Dom was flying back to his girlfriend in Australia, Rachel and Werner were heading further north, and Christian and Joe were on their way to Thailand. We'd shared some intense experiences and I felt as though I'd known them for years, not weeks.

I gave Rachel a huge hug goodbye: she had really grown on me. I could tell she was destined to do amazing things and would probably end up in some high-powered job in Washington. I was almost relieved to say goodbye to Dom. It was a torment having him close but out of reach.

Life on the Banana Pancake Trail was incredibly fun and I was sad to say goodbye to my friends. But I had been starting to feel as though I'd joined a youth group, which wasn't something I would ever do. Going to the palace had reminded me how much I loved the solitude of travelling alone. I was gaining confidence in myself as a traveller and had just about made up my mind to meet up with Tom in China. But first I needed to sample the banana pancakes in Vietnam.

10

HANOI HUSTLE

I stood stock still on the edge of the pavement as swarms of motorbikes whizzed past me in a blur of noise and colour. The sheer number of them was staggering. They ducked and weaved past one another without staying in a lane or heeding a red light – nor did the cars, bicycles or buses competing for space. There were so many horns honking at the same time that it almost blended into one long continuous honk, with orchestral backup from trilling bicycle bells and the guttural chug of diesel engines. I watched in disbelief as a motorbike carrying a father and his three kids cut across the traffic in a perpendicular direction.

I'd been standing there like a fool for five minutes while I tried to psyche myself up to cross the road. Trying to judge when there was an adequate break in the traffic was making my heart pound and my hands clammy, because there was no actual break. Yet no one else appeared flustered by the chaos. Many of the commuters wore smog masks, but the faces I could see looked positively serene.

Just do it.

I took a couple of tentative steps out onto the road and

almost had my foot run over by a motorbike that came up on my left. The driver swerved just in time and I leaped back onto the pavement.

I can't do it.

A wave of panic passed through me. My trip had literally come to a standstill, a hundred metres from my guesthouse in Hanoi.

Another couple of minutes passed, and then I hit upon an idea. When a young woman near me started to cross the road, I slipped into step with her. She ventured out into the traffic slowly but steadily, and at no point did she ever stop. This was an important first lesson: my instinct had been to dart onto the road, kamikaze style.

We reached the other side without incident and the young woman disappeared into the sea of people on the footpath, perhaps oblivious to the fact that I had been shadowing her. I was buoyed by the small achievement and decided to continue with the walking tour mapped out by my Lonely Planet after buying a ticket for the water puppet show that night.

I was back on the sidewalk with my head in my guidebook when a street hawker approached and started barking at me to buy a bunch of her bananas. She was wearing loose-fitting pyjamas and a conical hat. No wonder she wanted to offload some of the ripe yellow fruit – she was carrying two huge baskets of them on the ends of a bamboo shoulder pole.

'You take them,' she commanded.

Not knowing what to do, I swung around to face the other way and walked as quickly as I could without breaking into an actual jog for the sake of my dignity. I breathed a sigh of relief when I heard no further entreaties from the woman and assumed the heavy load slowed her down. I kept walking a little more just to be sure, and then took a seat on a low plastic stool at a food stall. I had the most incredible iced coffee in a long glass as I took in my atmospheric surrounds.

Hanoi's historic Old Quarter was unlike anything I'd ever seen. Every inch of space was occupied along its narrow streets, which criss-crossed an area that had served as a commercial hub for a thousand years. The bolthole stores seemed endless. Merchandise spilled out onto the pavement beside the parked scooters, was strung up from the awnings and stacked in tall piles. The apartments above the shops were a jumble of architectural styles: boxy flats with reflective glass windows were crammed in next to colonial-era buildings with peeling, butter-coloured paint; their French windows flung open and wispy plants growing out of ornate crevices. Even the birds were busy: sparrows fluttered from the branches of gnarled old trees to the thick web of powerlines and back again.

An old man pedalled past me with an enormous load of blue containers strapped to his bicycle. Then came a beat-up old car that cruised by at a snail's pace. It only just managed to squeeze through the narrow lane, but no one raised an eyebrow at its audacity.

Hanoi immediately struck me as a marvellous but intense city. As I zigzagged my way through the Old Quarter that morning, hawkers presented me with a dizzying array of consumer goods: t-shirts featuring Tintin and the red Vietnamese flag with its single yellow star, lipsticks, sunglasses, watercolour prints of rice paddies, smoking pots of food, musical instruments and counterfeit Rolexes.

I wanted to buy a couple of the things I was offered, but I was too intimidated to begin bargaining on my first day in the country. I hadn't got my head around the colourful new currency of dong that was sitting in my wallet. One Australian dollar was equal to about 13,000 dong, and my thirteen times tables were non-existent. The idea of using a calculator was laughable: it would expose me as easy prey for a massively inflated starting price.

After a lady selling war-propaganda posters came so close to my face that I had to wipe away little flecks of spit when she left, I took temporary refuge in a Buddhist temple. I entered it by crossing an elegant arched bridge, underneath which was a pond filled with koi. A lacquered white horse stood in the centre of the temple, which was flanked by enormous burgundy pillars. Small groups of people were praying in front of the grinning horse, and there were bouquets of dandelions and plates of green bananas left in front of it as offerings. Bunches of smoking incense sticks gave off a pleasant sandalwood scent. I wandered about the well-tended gardens, with massive pots of bonsai and topiary in the shape of birds and squirrels.

But no sooner had I returned to the street than a particularly persistent street hawker started trailing me. It was a big mistake to initially show interest in the t-shirt he offered me, which was emblazoned with the name of a movie I loved, *Good Morning, Vietnam*. I started to walk away, but the hawker darted in front of me. He was waving his arms while insisting his t-shirts were the cheapest in Hanoi. He seemed inexplicably angry with me: it wasn't so much an offer to buy from him as an accusation of failing to do so. I noticed that his face was twitching and I felt a bit uneasy. I tried to discourage him by saying that purple didn't suit me.

'What colour do you want? I have every colour,' he replied, and whipped out ten different shades in clear plastic packaging.

I had run out of excuses.

'I'll take the black one,' I said weakly.

Serene Laos felt like a distant memory. I ached to be back walking its sleepy streets.

AFTER A DELICIOUSLY LONG SLEEP, I took a cyclo to Ho Chi Minh's Mausoleum the next morning. I was dropped right out the front of the massive complex, where the complete absence of vehicles and street hawkers made strolling about a breeze. The guards dotted about the grounds on sentry duty didn't so much as glance in my direction. They stood to attention in all-white military uniforms that included gloves, a peaked cap and a gold sash. They must have been pouring sweat.

Cameras and bags weren't allowed inside the mausoleum, so I handed mine in and put the tag I was given in my back pocket. I skipped up the steps and took my place in the line inside the massive marble crypt. The lights were dimmed and it was as quiet as a library. Signs pointed out the various rules of decorum. No talking. No phones. No singlets or shorts. No hands in pockets.

Ho Chi Minh would be the second dead person I had ever seen. The memory of seeing my grandpa at his open-coffin funeral a few years earlier had burned itself into my brain.

There were a lot of tourists in the queue, who perhaps like me had been drawn there partly out of morbid curiosity. The majority of visitors were locals though, and I found it extraordinary that long lines of people wishing to pay their respects still formed daily, almost forty years after their leader's death. But then again, Ho Chi Minh was a national hero. No one before or since came close to his stature, which was almost mythical.

Ho Chi Minh had been a man of action, and spent his entire life fighting for his country's independence and sovereignty. In 1946 he forced the emperor to abdicate, thereby ending one hundred and forty-three years of the Vietnamese monarchy. He led the independence movement against the French colonialists, and persisted despite the odds of success seeming minuscule. The French were eventually defeated in battle and left in 1954, ending almost seventy years of colonial rule. Ho Chi Minh was prime minister for ten years and had been president for twenty-four years when he died in 1969. He didn't live to see his nation defeat Americans forces after twenty years of war, nor did he get to see his once-divided country reunified. The former capital of South Vietnam, Saigon, was renamed Ho Chi Minh City in his honour.

'Uncle Ho', as he was affectionately known, was also a journalist, poet, writer and polyglot. He was revered as much for the communist ideology he espoused as his victories in battle. Vietnam was still a communist country – along with Laos it was one of just a handful left in the world.

And yet I couldn't see any real-life evidence of communism. Vietnam was the most commerce-driven country I'd ever come across: the hustle had been turned into an art form. Ironically, the touts kept spruiking communist merchandise featuring the hammer and sickle symbols. I'd turned down key rings, t-shirts, coffee mugs, fridge magnets, tote bags and posters depicting agrarian scenes. Vietnam was a walking contradiction.

I was almost at the front of the line. I watched the two older women ahead of me look upon their former leader with solemn awe. They murmured a few words of prayer and made the sign of the cross before moving on.

I had about half a minute to take in the sight of this giant of history. Ho Chi Minh lay in repose inside a glass case, with his head resting on a velvet cushion and his face illuminated by the soft glow of a lamp. His eyes were closed and there was a faint smile on his lips. He was wearing his trademark khaki suit and I was close enough to make out the individual hairs of his long, wispy beard. His skin had a distinct yellowed tone and a waxy appearance.

It was hard to fathom that Ho Chi Minh had been lying there like that for decades. Apparently his final wish was to be cremated and have his ashes scattered over farming land as fertiliser. I felt sorry for him in a way because he was forever on display.

LUNCH WAS a spicy noodle soup called pho that came with tender pieces of diced beef, sliced sausage, knuckle bones and generous handfuls of mint, basil, shredded carrot, bok choy and bean sprouts. The combination of spicy, sour, sweet, and salty flavours in a single dish was a revelation, as was the fact that raw vegetables and cold noodles were delicious and filling. Food was the most immediately accessible aspect of Vietnamese culture. It was a delight.

I headed back to the guesthouse to buy a ticket for a two-night boat tour of Halong Bay, as I had promised the friendly boss of the family-run guesthouse that I would get my ticket from her. She was talking to another backpacker at the travel desk and smiled and waved me over to take a seat with them.

'Hi, Jess,' she said. 'This is Akihito from Japan. He's just back from Halong Bay and can tell you about it.'

As Akihito turned to face me, I saw he was wearing dark sunglasses, and then I noticed a cane leaning against his chair. He was vision impaired.

The three of us chatted for a few minutes. Akihito told me that he'd spent the past three weeks travelling the length of the country from his starting point of Ho Chi Minh City. When he cheerfully said that he'd had a ball, I was a bit lost for words. I wanted to ask Akihito how he managed to travel without being able to see, but I stopped myself. It would be a bit like him asking me how I got by as a solo female traveller – patronising. But it did occur to me that I was travelling through Vietnam without a disability and that I had the global language of

English as my first language – and yet I could scarcely cross the road without turning it into a massive deal.

'Enjoy Vietnam,' Akihito said as he excused himself to head out to Hoan Kiem Lake.

'I will,' I replied, and I meant it.

Those ten minutes with Akihito changed my outlook. Vietnam was intense, but I would be okay. Actually, I would be better than okay.

In the late afternoon, I took a pew on a low plastic stool at a bia hoi stall in an alleyway. Hanoi was famous for its bia hoi, which translates to 'fresh beer'. As I sipped my second glass, I exchanged a smile with the backpacker sitting at the table opposite me. He had been served a fresh glass of bia hoi at the same time as I was. He was a broad-shouldered guy with a goatee, tattoos and a red bandana around his head. He was wearing a Ramones t-shirt and looked like a bit of a badass. He invited me to sit with him and soon had me laughing at his recollections of some of the bizarre backpackers he'd come across over the past couple of months. There was a guy who wore a scarf so long that it dragged along the ground and another who barked like a dog after too many beers. Robert had a wry sense of humour and a cool Californian accent.

We munched on grilled pork patties as the waiters darted about replenishing their patrons' drinks and taking tall stacks of empties out the back. One waiter sat on a chair and was constantly filling glass mugs from a hose connected to a steel keg. Bia hoi is a light beer that is brewed overnight and delivered every morning to establishments across Hanoi. It has no preservatives, so it has a shelf life of just twenty-four hours.

We'd had about four rounds of bia hoi when a backpacker called Jane stopped as she was walking past and asked if she could join us. She was in a bit of a state as she'd just realised she'd been scammed.

'My flight from Bangkok got in at around ten last night,' she began in her thick Scottish accent. 'I asked a cab driver to take me to Manh Dung Guesthouse, which I'd chosen from my guidebook. He told me it had closed down, but his uncle had a place close to it that was a little bit more expensive but had better rooms. I said fine – I mean, I had no choice. The rooms were rubbish. Plus there were cockroaches in the shared bathrooms. And just before I came here, I walked past Manh Dung Guesthouse – it's just over there.'

We nodded as Jane took a big sip of her beer.

'I went in to ask if they have a room available and I told the woman on the desk what happened. She told me that Hanoi has a taxi and hotel mafia group who are always trying to steal their guests. The cab driver would get paid a commission for taking me to the other guesthouse. I'm going to move my stuff there tomorrow because I've already paid for tonight at the other place.'

'Maybe don't confront them about it when you check out,' I suggested. 'There's a warning in Lonely Planet about not getting angry. They've had letters from backpackers about people getting aggressive with them after they refused to buy a tour or stay at a certain hotel. Their advice is just to back away slowly to avoid the situation turning nasty.'

'Okay,' said Jane reluctantly. 'I guess it's not worth getting into a fight about it. They are cheats though.'

'Without a doubt,' Robert sympathised. 'I think it's a dog-eat-dog society in Hanoi, though. My guesthouse manager told me that a new guesthouse just opened down the road with the exact same name as hers, which is listed in Lonely Planet and really popular. Apparently the police do nothing to stop them ripping off her business – there's no such thing as copyright law in Vietnam. There's no social welfare either. Got no money? You starve.

Your kids starve. So I guess people will do whatever they can to get by, even if it means being dishonest.'

'I agree,' I said. 'People just have to hustle.'

As if on cue, a beggar came up to our table and shook an upturned conical hat at us with an exaggerated expression of sorrow. Robert gave him a few thousand dong.

'Should we have another round?' he asked.

'Sure,' said Jane. 'It's not exactly breaking the bank. And it's definitely taken the edge off.'

Bia hoi was believed to be the cheapest beer in the world. At ten cents a glass, we could sit there drinking all night long and it would only cost us a few bucks each. And that is exactly what we did.

OVER THE NEXT few days in Hanoi, I noticed that some backpackers weren't as reasonable as Jane or as empathetic as Robert. I came across some who were outright rude towards locals. While having beers with a few backpackers that I'd met at the guesthouse, a French guy sitting opposite me swatted away a street kid as though she were a fly in his food. He continued talking and laughing as the little girl slunk away with her empty baseball cap, looking crestfallen. I fought back the urge to tell him that he had a winning lottery ticket in life, not because he deserved it, but by virtue of where he happened to be born and the fact that it gave him an EU passport.

While aboard the boat in stunning Halong Bay, I met an Israeli who complained incessantly. He kept harping on about having to pay for his drinking water, which was so cheap that it seemed an absurd thing to get upset about. The young tour operator just kept politely telling him that water wasn't included in the cost of the tour package, and that she would pass on his feedback to her boss. I wondered how much rubbish she had to put up with at work.

It was clear the UNESCO World Heritage-listed site was also putting up with a lot of rubbish – literally. Mass tourism was bringing in tonnes of it. The trash cans at some of the karst cave entrances were overflowing and when we went kayaking I saw beer cans and other detritus bobbing about. At night, the dozen or so anchored boats pumped out sewerage into the emerald-green waters.

Some aspects of the backpacker scene in Vietnam were depressing and I contemplated cutting my time there short and making a beeline for China. In the end I decided to stay on as planned because I'd already arranged to meet up with a Vietnamese family in Ho Chi Minh City who were related to a friend in Melbourne. I'd also contacted the manager of an orphanage about possibly doing some volunteering. I didn't want to cancel either.

So I took the bus to the much smaller city of Hui, which was ancient and enchanting. After a couple of days I continued south to Hoi An by bus. It was a short but eventful journey. I was sitting next to a Vietnamese man who told me how he and his parents and eight siblings had fled from the communist north to the south in 1954, just before Vietnam was divided for the next twenty years. When the country was reunified, he, his wife and one year-old child fled from the horrors of the war. They arrived in Malaysia by boat and spent many miserable years there in refugee camps, before finally being granted asylum in Canada. He was back in Vietnam for the first time in a decade and was on his way to see relatives, so it was a very emotional journey.

Liem taught me the word for a very cheap guesthouse called *nha nghi* that was only ever advertised in Vietnamese. He patiently corrected me as I repeated the word 'nha nghi' after him until he was confident I could say it properly. Then he taught me a couple of helpful phrases, including how to say, 'This meal was delicious.'

Towards the end of the journey, I got chatting to the Vietnamese girl behind me. Bich was travelling back home after a weekend in Hanoi with her Irish boyfriend, Ben, who seemed a nice, unassuming guy who stared at his girlfriend adoringly. Bich was stunning – I got distracted as she spoke while inwardly marvelling at her features and long glossy hair. I could only imagine the effect she had on men. She gave me the names of the best places to get clothes tailored, which is what the city's artisans were famous for, and invited me out for dinner that night with her sister, Ben and some other friends.

At dinner, Bich told me that she and her friends were having a get together the next day, which happened to be my three-month travel anniversary. I liked to mark it on the first day of each month by doing something even more memorable than usual, and a beach party with locals would be amazing. I was in high spirits as I showered and got ready. There was something about Vietnam that had got under my skin. I was pleased I could cross the road and hold my own with a hawker, and I knew what 100,000 dong would get me. I had even mastered a few phrases in Vietnamese.

When I turned up there were about ten others at the restaurant, which was a beach shack only a couple of hundred metres from the shore. Myself, Ben and another Irish guy were the only foreigners there. We played a couple of rounds of pool and a few of us went for a swim and bodysurfed on the small waves. Back under the shade of the hut, icy-cold beers and grilled snacks kept arriving. I couldn't stop smiling and told Bich that they were showing me paradise.

One of Bich's friends had brought his guitar and a married couple had their baby boy with them. He was content being passed around and cuddled as we listened to the guitarist's beautifully mellow voice. When Bich's sister gave the boy to me, I put him on my lap and softly jiggled my legs. He turned to look up at me with eyes like pools of liquid chocolate – and my heart melted when he broke into a grin.

Just then an enormous fish was brought to our table. It had been cooked just as it was caught, with its scales and fins still on and eyeballs intact. Bich used chopsticks to peel back the crispy skin and load my plate. It had been sautéed in a spicy, garlicky sauce with diced capsicums and watercress and was incredibly tasty paired with fluffy rice. I realised I had the perfect opportunity to try out the phrase I'd been taught by the nice man on the bus.

'I have something I'd like to say in Vietnamese,' I said.

'Good for you,' said Bich. 'Tell us.'

I repeated the phrase about the food being delicious.

Bich burst out laughing. The guy next to her stopped chewing and held his fork in the air. The others were looking at me strangely.

'What?' I said, puzzled.

'I don't think...' Bich started laughing again. She paused for a couple of seconds as she composed herself enough to finish the sentence. 'I don't think you said it right. You just told us that you're really horny.'

11

BAD BACKPACKERS

I was resigned to the fact that overnight buses were part of the deal as a backpacker. The only way to avoid them was a waste of time and money: it meant breaking up the journey by spending a night somewhere I wasn't actually interested in visiting. It was better to just push through on an overnight bus and catch up on missed sleep the following day. I was also discovering an unexpected upside of an extra-long journey: sometimes it became a bonding experience.

The first part of the twelve-hour bus ride from Hoi An to the coastal city of Nha Trang passed relatively quickly. I was sitting next to a Vietnamese girl who fell asleep shortly after we pulled out of the bus depot, so I listened to music and stared out the window at the beautiful coastline as dusk fell. The bus travelled for over three hours before making its first roadside stop – by which time I was absolutely busting to go to the toilet.

I hurried past the hot-food stalls to make a beeline for the toilet blocks out the back. A haggard older woman sat at a table with a tin moneybox and a sign indicating that the fee to use the toilet was 2000 dong, which was the equivalent of about five cents. I'd never paid to use a toilet before, but my need was so urgent I would have paid much more. I handed her the money and walked along a short, dark passageway that opened into a small room of communal toilets. I was hit by an overwhelming stench of raw sewerage and started breathing through my mouth rather than my nostrils.

There were no cubicles to provide privacy to those using the dozen or so squat toilets, which consist of a hole in the ground rather than a toilet seat. Women of all shapes and sizes were crouched down beside one another like dudes at a urinal (except that men would be standing facing the wall and the women in this room were backed up against it).

I went over to a vacant toilet and put my feet on the stained ceramic tiles on either side of the hole in the ground. My pee splattered over my feet and ankles and my fisherman pants got wet from scraping the filthy ground. I felt self-conscious and stared straight ahead as the woman next to me washed herself with a small bucket of water scooped from a nearby trough. Toilet paper wasn't used in Southeast Asia, so I carried my own tissues and used a little bucket to flush the paper down the drain in the floor. I was relieved in more ways than one when I was out of there.

When the bus stopped at another highway rest stop a couple of hours later, I expected the toilets to be similar and mentally prepared myself as I took my place in the queue. Behind me was a backpacker I recognised from a boat cruise in Hoi An, although I couldn't remember her name. We exchanged a smile and started chatting, and she reintroduced herself as Romi from Sydney. When it was almost my turn for the toilet, she jokingly wished me good luck. At least these squat toilets had side partitions, even if they were only hip height and lacked a door.

'Hey, um, Jess – do you have any toilet paper?' Romi called out from the stall beside me.

'No I don't, sorry. I just used my last. I meant to buy more tissues at the last rest stop but I forgot. Oh wait! I've got something else you could use. Just give me a second.' I unzipped my day pack and took out my book and tore out a few pages. It was an old Penguin classic, with reasonably absorbent paper. It was a grossly disrespectful way to treat a biography of India's first prime minister. 'Use this as toilet paper, Romi. And don't worry – I've read that chapter,' I said as I passed the pages over the top of the stall.

'Oh gosh – treating a book this way is sacrilege,' said Romi with an astonished laugh. 'But thank you.'

Afterwards, Romi and I walked over to the tables at the meals area and she introduced me to the guy she was sitting next to on the bus. Adam from Ireland had been on the boat tour in Hoi An as well, and I remembered thinking that they were both funny and nice. We told Adam how we'd used book pages as toilet paper and that got us talking about what we'd been reading lately. Romi loved books and writing as much as I did. We happily made a plan to stay at the same guesthouse in Nha Trang and then filed back onto the bus.

The rest of the journey passed in a thickening fog of fatigue. I only managed to sleep for an hour or two and grew demented with fantasies about lying flat. It was about seven o'clock in the morning when the bus pulled into the depot in Nha Trang, which is about two thirds of the way down Vietnam's elongated S-shaped territory.

Romi, Adam and I had just retrieved our backpacks from the storage section of the bus when a girl came up to us.

'Do you guys know somewhere to stay?' she asked with a sunny smile and an American accent. 'And uh, would you mind if I tagged along?'

'Sure,' replied Romi. 'We're going to a place that's three dollars for a single room and it's right by the beach.'

'That sounds neat. Thanks a lot.' She beamed. 'I'm Paula

from Nevada. I didn't see any other backpackers on the bus and hoped you wouldn't mind if I just walked right up and asked if I could join you.'

Americans often had a confidence about them that I admired. They didn't waste time being too shy to ask for what they wanted.

The four of us chatted away as we walked towards the guesthouse. We all said how god-awful tired we were and compared how little sleep we thought we'd got on the bus.

'My eyes feel so hot and dry, and speaking coherently is a struggle,' I whined.

We had all checked in and had our room keys in our hands when Adam said, 'I know we all feel like shit. But does anyone feel like going to the beach? You know, just to see what it looks like. And then we could come back here and crash and go out again later this afternoon.'

Adam had a mischievous glint in his eyes, which made his eyebrow ring all the more fetching. He was bronzed, broad-shouldered and an incredible hunk.

'I'm in,' said Romi without a moment's hesitation.

'Me too,' added Paula.

'Me three,' I said. 'Let's put our bathers on and meet out the front in five minutes.'

As I got changed, I laughed to myself as I realised that my fear of missing out on any fun was stronger than my urge to sleep, even when I was deliriously tired. Plus it was a beautifully sunny day and the ocean was only a couple of hundred metres away.

I took one look at Nha Trang's stunning beach and knew that staying up was the right call. The turquoise waters were interspersed with the white foam of breaking waves, and verdant mountains hugged the gently curved coastline. Swaying palms were dotted about the powder-white sand and no sooner were the silky soft grains squeaking between my toes than a hawker was dashing towards us with beach lounges under her arms. The price she quoted to hire them was so cheap that we immediately agreed. She set up the four lounges under thatched umbrellas in less than a minute and was then off to find her next customers.

A second hawker approached with a blue cooler box. A handkerchief was tied under her conical hat, leaving only a narrow gap for her to see out. It was a typically hot and humid day, but she was wearing a long-sleeved shirt, trousers, gloves, and socks underneath her flip-flops. Pale skin was considered a mark of sophistication and wealth in Vietnam, whereas a suntan was for paupers. The woman kneeled on the sand and opened the cooler box. Inside were cans of Heineken, Budweiser, Tiger and Corona lying on a bed of ice and dripping with condensation.

'It's only eight o'clock in the morning, so why do those beers look so good?' said Adam, licking his lips.

'Well, because we've hardly slept it kind of feels like it's late in the night,' I said. 'Let's have a beer and a swim and then go back to the guesthouse to crash.'

But we never did go back to the guesthouse that morning. The first round of beers gave us a second wind, which led to us having second, third and fourth rounds. Other hawkers descended upon us carrying delicious breakfast foods, so we filled our bellies with hash browns, bacon and slices of mango and watermelon. One hawker even came up to us with a basket of live lobsters and offered to cook one in front of us on her portable steamer. We said no to the lobster, but yes to a massage from two other hawkers. Paula and I went first. We lay face down on a towel in the sand and unclipped the backs of our bikinis. I was enjoying the pleasant sensations of the massage as I listened to Romi and Adam chat about the girl Adam had been sleeping with in Hoi An. He liked Jacquie and she was Irish too, but he hadn't set off travelling with the intention of ending up in a relationship. He was on the fence about it.

Suddenly there was a bang not far from my face and sand scattered as though from an invisible kick.

'Holy shit!' said Adam, laughing. 'My lighter exploded!'

'Wow! I guess it overheated in the sun,' said Paula, brushing the sand off her slim thighs.

Within seconds, two hawkers were competing for Adam's business to replace the busted lighter.

Romi gleefully moved onto the sand for her massage and I took her place on the banana lounge.

'I could get used to this,' she said, wriggling a little on the towel to get comfortable. 'I feel positively regal.'

By lunchtime the beach had filled up and there wasn't a free umbrella in sight. There was a light breeze and a cloudless sky, and someone was playing Vietnamese pop music from a nearby stereo. We clinked our cans as we embarked on what was possibly our sixth round.

'I can see why Nha Trang has a reputation for being a party town,' I said. 'It's practically impossible not to party here.'

'Resistance is futile,' agreed Paula with a wink.

Romi and I grabbed a couple of rubber rings and went swimming. Adam and Paula kicked back with another beer and minded our stuff. A young girl was swimming nearby with her family, and Romi made her laugh by making a wig out of seaweed. Romi and the girl held hands as the waves crashed over them and chased each other on the shore. I tried to catch some waves while straddling my rubber ring, but mostly just swallowed a heap of salt water. The ocean was so refreshing that my fatigue evaporated.

I had just dried off when a young local guy walked past us towards the shore in the distinctly non-beach attire of black trousers and a white shirt. He must have been at a wedding or formal event – he was wasted. We watched open-mouthed as he walked into the water fully clothed. He shook his spiky hair dramatically and pumped his fists in the air. Other swimmers were laughing and joking with him. After a few minutes, he came back out and pranced and danced to the music playing on the stereo. I couldn't stop laughing as he posed in his soaking wet clothes with his white shirt knotted at the waist like a teenage girl.

The day passed with more beers, more swims and the swapping of life stories. Every now and again, the lounge lady came and helped us move our things further up as the tide came in, and we paid her a bit of extra dong for doing so.

And then, somehow, dusk was falling. Romi, Paula, Adam and I went back to the guesthouse for a shower. However, the epic drinking session wasn't over – we were heading back out to an Aussie-run nightspot called the Sailing Club for dinner.

Along the way we passed an open-air restaurant with a wedding in full swing. We stood there watching the guests busting moves on the dance floor, and a guy waved at us to come and join them. We were given beers and did the macarena. Then we took some photos with the wedding party as though we were all old friends, before continuing on our way.

We settled into some lounges at the beachside bar, which had pool tables and foosball. We ordered a couple of plates of potato wedges to soak up the alcohol, and also ordered another round of beers.

'You're really sunburnt, Romi,' said Paula. 'You are too, Jess. Does it hurt?'

'I can't feel it,' replied Romi with a grin and a little hiccup.

'Do I look like that red lobster at the beach?' I asked while pretending my arms were clacking pincers.

'Or a broken robot?' said Adam.

I hit him affectionately. We started laughing. Everything was fun and funny. I plaited two pigtails in Paula's beautifully silky hair and Romi took off Adam's striped bandana and put it over her soft dark curls. Then we took a heap of photos of each other as we hugged and pulled dumb faces. We kept saying it had been one of the best days of our lives, and vowed to somehow always stay friends.

Adam and I went to get more drinks and on the way he spotted an erotic Hindu bas relief. He went over to it. He pinched one of its nipples and looked back at me with come-hither eyes and his tongue poked out suggestively. Laughing, I took photos of him. Then we swapped places and I copied the statue's pose, which was a bit like the one-legged tree pose in yoga. My balance was off and I fell over. Adam gave me an arm up and I started laughing and couldn't stop. Then he started laughing so hard his face turned red and his voice came out squeaky. We laughed even harder.

We were being bad backpackers – the ones that made me cringe when I saw them because they were so obnoxious. But like all bad backpackers, we were so wasted we just thought we were hilarious.

Late into the night, one by one, we fell quiet and subdued. We started to wobble our way home along the footpath. Paula had her arm around me, and Adam and Romi were singing a Smashing Pumpkins song up ahead.

What occurred next seemed to happen so fast I couldn't take it in. A motorcycle came up from behind and mounted the pavement. The guy sitting behind the driver leaned out and yanked at Romi's shoulder bag. It came off with a violent jerk and she fell to the ground. The motorbike sped off.

'Oh my god!' I shouted.

'Shit!' shouted Adam, who sprinted off in pursuit of the thieves.

Romi got back up on her feet, kicked off her flip-flops and followed him.

Paula and I just looked at each other for a few seconds, dumbfounded. Then Paula picked up Romi's shoes and we headed after them.

We found Adam and Romi a couple of minutes later. They were doubled over trying to catch their breath.

'The motherfuckers went down an alleyway and I lost sight of them,' said Adam.

'Well, maybe it's lucky you didn't catch up with them,' I said. 'They might have been carrying a knife or some other weapon.'

'Romi, are you okay?' Paula asked. 'Are you hurt?'

'I'm okay,' Romi replied, but she looked shaken.

'What was in your bag?' I asked.

'My phone and camera. About three hundred dollars. My bank cards.'

'Oh no,' I said. 'I'm so sorry. What a pair of arseholes.'

'Oh my god,' Romi added in a small voice. Despite being insanely sunburnt, the colour drained from her face. 'Earlier the woman on reception gave me back my passport. I usually keep it in my backpack but I couldn't be bothered going to my room again so I just stuffed it in my handbag. I've lost my passport.'

12

DING DONG

Romi got up at six o'clock the next morning and went to the local police station, where she filed a report about being mugged. The policeman gave no indication there was a chance of getting her stuff back – thefts were an everyday occurrence. But at least now she could lodge a travel insurance claim. Then she phoned the Australian embassy in Hanoi and was told it would take a few weeks to issue her with an emergency replacement passport. Romi would have to remain in Vietnam until it was ready. Her travel plans had gone out the window.

Along with being completely stressed out, Romi also had a crushing hangover and the worst sunburn of all four of us. I tried to put antiseptic cream on the festering blisters on her back, but she yelped out in pain so much I had to stop. We laid very low that next day.

Adam decided to meet up with Jacquie somewhere and bid us farewell. Paula and I lent Romi some money to tide her over until the replacement bank cards arrived, and then took a bus four hours south to Mui Ne Beach. Romi hoped to catch us up in Ho Chi Minh City as soon as she could.

Paula and I were pretty down about what had happened to Romi and it was hard to summon any enthusiasm for Mui Ne Beach. It was windy and the surf was too big for safe swimming. The town was so spread out that it was hard to get around on foot. We moved on to Ho Chi Minh City after a couple of nights.

Vietnam's commercial capital wasn't an attractive city like the actual capital of Hanoi. Every inch of Saigon – as everyone seemed to call it – was carpeted in concrete, which matched the persistently overcast sky. The architecture was mostly modern and soulless. But the change of pace was just what I needed. Saigon was a city that demanded my full attention. The energy of its 8 million citizens was palpable and everything seemed to move at a frenetic pace. Crossing the ten-lane roads was an adventure sport. I preferred jumping on the back of a motorcycle taxi, as I was free to absorb the sights and smells while the driver decided how best to navigate congestion that suddenly made Hanoi seem like a quaint rural town.

One of the first things I planned on doing in Saigon was to email my dad's friend, Les, to let him know I was in town. He was an expat in Saigon and I'd known him since I was a kid. He and Dad were friends through their work in the furniture industry, and whenever he'd phoned up Dad and I'd answered the landline he'd ask me how school was going and we'd have a bit of a chat. I'd met Les a few times when I'd tagged along with Dad on his sales calls to furniture shops. I remembered him as friendly and funny, although it was probably at least five years since we had spoken.

I emailed Les and asked if he was free to meet up. Then I set off to explore the city with Paula.

The two of us got happily lost inside the labyrinth of stalls at Ben Thanh market, which is one of the city's biggest. It seemed to sell everything under the sun, and had rows of stores bursting to the seams with fake designer handbags, sunglasses, shoes and jeans. I bought a military-style dog-tag necklace from a corner stall selling all kinds of war memorabilia and souvenirs, which were no doubt mostly fakes too.

'How do they even...?' exclaimed Paula, turning over a bottle of pale yellow rice wine with a dead cobra and scorpion inside. The cobra had somehow been frozen stiff with its fangs bared and the tail of the twice unlucky scorpion inside its mouth.

'Yikes,' I said. 'Imagine if the glass broke.'

We each bought anklets and a pair of low heels with straps embellished with brightly coloured beads. The soles were made of varnished wood and were surprisingly comfortable. I put them on right away.

We continued walking until we came to a nail salon with a line of women sitting out the front getting pedicures. The manicurists sat on little plastic stools, absorbed in their work. I'd never had a pedicure before and excitedly browsed a catalogue of nail art designs. I chose a black base with orange, white and yellow flowers. We put our feet up and chatted away as the women got to work.

'My feet have never looked better,' I said as I admired my freshly painted toenails, deeply tanned feet, new shoes and anklet.

'The shopping is so good in Vietnam,' said Paula. 'Everything is so cheap and well made.'

'I've bought things I didn't even know I needed,' I agreed. 'But my pack is going to explode if I try to put one more thing in it.'

No sooner were the words out of my mouth than a lady carrying an enormous stack of books caught my eye. I asked if she had Lonely Planet's *China* and she nodded, and set the pile down on the ground. It was almost as tall as she was. She unfastened the stretchy bandages around the pile and handed me the book.

A frisson of excitement passed through me as I flicked through its pages and saw photos of the country I was about to see with my own eyes. Judging from the faintness of the type, the book was a pirated photocopy of the original. It was also twice as heavy as any guidebook I'd had previously. Of course, that made sense: China was a massive country. I handed over 300,000 dong and the hawker walked away with a slightly lighter load.

When I next checked my emails, there was a reply from Les. He was free to meet up and – to my surprise – he was also offering me a place to stay.

If you need a bed, we have a spare suite.
    No charge – can wash your clothes and all that.
    Have a maid. The offer is there.
    Call me.
    Les

I loved the solitude of a cheap hotel room, but seeing Romi get mugged had been scary and I'd been on my guard ever since. The idea of staying at someone's home and being able to relax was appealing. Plus Paula was about to catch a flight to Japan and Romi was still killing time in Nha Trang.

I continued mulling over the offer from Les while I replied to an email from my good friend Gavin. We'd been friends since practically the first day of law school, some seven years ago. There was a possibility we could have been more than friends, but we had never been single at the same time. To be more precise: Gavin almost always had a girlfriend.

When Matthew broke up with me and I was devastated, Gavin spent ages trying to cheer me up. We'd talk for ages on the phone, or he'd convince me to come out with some friends to the Mountain View Pub (which we dubbed 'Mountain Spew' because everyone, including us, always got wasted there).

The last time I saw Gavin before leaving for Cambodia, I'd told him that I'd realised it was lucky Matthew had dumped me, because I was free to enjoy what I jokingly referred to as my 'sexual safari' across Asia. In his email, Gavin had asked me how things were going on that front. Admittedly, there wasn't much to tell him. I explained that Dario was still the only person I had slept with, and then continued:

I'M STILL SEARCHING for a one-night stand, but there have been some pretty weird complications. A couple of times I've bumped into the guy I almost had a thing with at some previous town I was in. We smile politely and talk about the weather!!

I FINISHED the email to Gavin by asking how his new squeeze was going, and then I hit send. To my horror, I realised I had somehow sent the email to Les as well as to Gavin.

'No, no, noooo,' I exclaimed so loudly that the girl at the computer next to me looked at me askance.

I bashed out a second email to Les asking him to ignore the first one. I also thanked him for the offer and said I would call him right away to ask whether I could come and stay the following day.

'How embarrassing,' I muttered under my breath as I left the internet cafe.

THE INCREDIBLY LOUD ding dong of the doorbell had scarcely finished chiming when a tiny young woman appeared. She beamed and said a few words of welcome in Vietnamese. Once inside the living room, she gave me a hand with my backpack as I removed it, and then motioned for me to take a seat on a nearby couch with a glass-topped coffee table and a stack of magazines. Another woman appeared and told me in perfect English that she was Annie, Les' secretary – they worked out of the ground floor, while Les lived on the second floor and I would be staying on the third. Les was due back any minute from a factory visit.

The woman who answered the door was introduced to me as Hue, the maid. She was standing in front of me holding a pair of slippers. I watched in disbelief as she kneeled down and undid the Velcro straps of my sandals. She gently removed my shoes and put the slippers on me. Then she went over to a table and tipped an enormous bottle of Johnnie Walker whisky that sat in a cradle. Still beaming and half bowing, she handed me a glass of Scotch.

'Thank you,' I said, taking a nip before she padded off to the kitchen.

Annie hadn't skipped a beat in our conversation, so I assumed my first exchange with a maid was normal. We chatted away happily for a few minutes before Les walked in the door.

'Look at you, Jess! You've grown up a lot since the last time I saw you,' he exclaimed after giving me a big hug.

He stood back to look at me, and we grinned at each other. Other than being tanned and having deeper crow's feet, Les looked pretty much the same to me, with his sandy hair and lanky frame.

Hue came over with a glass of whisky for Les. He leaned back into the couch and lit a cigarette with a satisfied sigh.

Annie said goodbye and headed home, where her three-year-old daughter and husband were waiting for her.

I was getting a buzz from the whisky as Les told me about his furniture business. He was exporting to about five different countries and was considering diversifying into scooters. Les had moved to Vietnam from Melbourne three years earlier. I knew he had separated from his wife around this time, but Dad hadn't told me any details.

As always, Les wanted to know about me. I said that I had managed to finish my law degree although, much to Dad's disappointment, I wasn't keen on pursuing a legal career.

'Being a lawyer just seems so boring to me, but I have no idea what I'm going to do when I finish travelling,' I said with a shrug. 'All I know is that I plan to live in London for a few years. Of course, I've got a British passport thanks to Dad being born there.'

'Work in general is kind of boring, most of the time,' said Les. 'But it's the only way to make a dollar so that you can travel and do all the things you love doing.'

'I guess that's true,' I said.

I told Les how I'd gone to an orphanage called the Sunshine School that morning because I was interested in helping kids in some kind of way. The cheerful American manager had shown me around the bright and colourful building, where I saw teeny tiny babies, a kindergarten and a section for kids with disabilities. There was an older boy there with cerebral palsy who was sort of writhing around in a cot, and he dribbled and grinned at me as I walked past. I couldn't get that image out of my mind.

I wanted to help the children and I'd hoped I had the fortitude to do so, however the minimum term for volunteers at the Sunshine School was six months. This was to try to prevent making any abandonment issues worse. Remaining in Ho Chi Minh City for that long would mean seeing far less of Asia than

I'd hoped to during my year-long travels and I didn't think I could make the commitment. The manager had told me about an orphanage in Mongolia that was also funded by the Christina Noble Foundation, and it permitted shorter volunteering stints. I was keen to do it after spending a month in China.

'Gosh,' said Les. 'I know why I stick to business. Seeing those orphans every day would get me down.'

We started talking about China, as Les was recently back from a business trip there. Hue then reappeared to let us know that dinner was ready.

'Do you want to head out for drinks after we eat? I know a couple of good bars,' Les said.

'I'd love to,' I replied.

'Okay great. Let's have some fun tonight, Jess. And let's make a deal that what happens in Vietnam stays in Vietnam. Does that sound good to you?' Les grinned and looked at me suggestively.

'Uh yes, sure,' I stuttered, smiling uneasily.

My mind was racing as I followed Hue up the stairs to my room. Had Les just meant that we wouldn't tell Dad how much we partied? It was possible – my dad was pretty straitlaced. Or was Les implying something else? I berated myself once more for sending that slutty-sounding email to him by mistake.

'Wow,' I exclaimed as Hue switched on the light.

The suite was enormous – Les must have been making some serious dong. There was a queen-size bed with a burgundy satin bedspread, a massive television and a gleaming ensuite. But what delighted me most was the desk and chair in the far corner where I could write my diary. A double door opened up to a vast rooftop area. I peered down at the chaos of a big intersection below before returning to the cool and quiet suite.

Suddenly I heard Les' voice coming up the stairs, 'You ready, Mudditt?'

I laughed and called back that I was. It had been such a long time since anyone had addressed me by my surname. It was a nickname many of male friends had given me at highschool.

'THE DRINKS ARE ON THE HOUSE,' said the bartender with a grin as he set down two martinis in front of us.

'Thanks, Andy,' said Les as he twizzled an olive on a toothpick before popping it in his mouth.

Andy was a friendly New Yorker and the owner of the bar, which was called Bottom Line. He towered over his female bar staff, who wore pink tank tops and darted about carrying frosted jugs of beer and replacing used ashtrays.

We were soon joined by Les' business partner, Clive, who dazzled me with card tricks. We moved to a table and another friend of Les' arrived – he was a smooth-talking pilot. A couple of other expat businessmen joined, and each time Les introduced me as the daughter of his friend, Simon. To my relief, I was getting no weird vibes from him whatsoever.

We'd been there about an hour when an attractive, well-dressed Vietnamese woman came and planted a kiss on Les' cheek before taking the seat next to me.

'Hey, Yen. Glad you could get away from work. Jess, this is Yen, my girlfriend.'

I shouldn't even have worried that Les might be a sleaze bag.

At around ten o'clock we went to a nightclub called Apocalypse Now, which was named after the classic war film starring Marlon Brando. It was a sort of dark bunker with flashes of neon strobes and thumping dance music. Yen and I had a dance with her friends while Les knocked back another round of beers with his mates. I was glad to be wearing my new heels but was still conscious of looking pretty daggy next to the beautiful Vietnamese women I was with in figure-hugging dresses.

Our final stop was a karaoke bar in a five star hotel. We flicked through a laminated catalogue of songs and took turns punching in the song number we wanted with a remote control. The lyrics came up on the screen with a sappy video clip playing in the background. After Les' friends sang a couple of rock songs, Yen and I took the microphones and sung 'My Heart Will Go On' from the *Titanic* soundtrack. It was grossly beyond my abilities as a singer and I was laughing so hard in parts that all I could get out was a whisper.

As I watched Les belt out Frank Sinatra's classic hit 'My Way', I thought how different he was from my dad, who I had never even seen drunk. Les was the life of the party and he was generous too: he kept telling me to put my dong away whenever I tried to buy a round of drinks.

'Your dad would be horrified, Jess,' he said with a laugh as he, Yen and I hailed a cab home a little after three in the morning.

∼

LES' apartment was an ideal base for sightseeing because it was within walking distance of most major tourist sites. I met up with Romi and we explored the Notre-Dame Cathedral and Independence Palace together, and had happy-hour drinks at a cheap and cheerful backpacker bar on a rainy afternoon. Despite having been stuck in the capital for who knows how long while she waited for a new passport, I found Romi remarkably chipper and wonderful company.

I spent a sombre morning alone at the War Remnants Museum, which was set up to document the atrocities committed by American troops against the Vietnamese people. I strolled in past the tanks, helicopters and jets parked out the front. There were quite a lot of tourists taking photographs in front of the war armoury.

As I wandered through the three-storey building, it struck me that America was willing to do anything to stop the spread of communism. I couldn't understand why it was considered so harmful, and to be stopped at all costs. Over the course of the twenty-year war, the American government sent more than 3 million troops to fight the Vietnamese communists of North Vietnam. The communists were led by Ho Chi Minh and known by the translated term of 'Vietcong' or just 'VC'. The museum plaques referred to the war not as the Vietnam War but as the 'American War'. Of course, that made sense.

None of what I saw was easy viewing, but it was the photography exhibition that hit me hardest. There were black-and-white photos of people who had been hit by napalm bombs and chemical herbicides such as Agent Orange. I saw people with skin that was charred to a crisp, babies with terrible deformities and a pile of bodies lying in a crumpled heap following the My Lai Massacre of 1968.

One photo took a few seconds for me to comprehend. An American soldier was holding up what looked like a big slab of steak – like something you'd feed a lion. Then I realised it was the remains of a corpse – a head, neck and arm. The Vietnamese man's legs and half his torso was strewn across the ground. The soldier was looking at the corpse with cool detachment, and in his other hand was an AK-47. I walked away feeling profoundly disturbed by the brutality human beings were capable of inflicting on one another.

I took a motorcycle taxi to Binh Soup Shop, which had doubled as the secret headquarters of the VC in Saigon. I ate a bowl of pho and read in my Lonely Planet how it was from right where I sat that the VC planned the Tet Offensive of 1968. The series of surprise attacks targeted places like the American embassy and Radio Saigon, and it made Americans back home wake up to the fact that they were not winning the war, and that the scale of suffering was immense.

'One has to wonder how many US soldiers ate here, completely unaware that the staff were all VC infiltrators,' stated my guidebook.

The next day I took a minibus out to the Cu Chi tunnels, where I and a dozen other tourists were shown around an area where a two-hundred-and-fifty-kilometre network of underground tunnels had been built by the VC. It stretched all the way to Cambodia.

We peered down at the living quarters, where people spent months at a time. Some parts of the tunnels had electricity, but mostly the inhabitants were guided by paraffin lamps. When they cooked, the smoke from the kitchens was channelled along vents so that it wafted out at an isolated spot much further away to prevent detection. The underground facilities included weapons factories, hospitals, command centres, schools and even theatres.

We took turns sliding into an open tunnel that was concealed with a trap door covered in leaves. I winced at a booby trap that would impale its animal or human victim on a bed of nails.

Part of a tunnel had been widened to accommodate tourists, but even so it was still tiny to crawl through, at just over a metre high and eighty centimetres wide. The girl in front of me went down but came back out in less than a minute because she got claustrophobic. I had to stifle my own rising sense of panic as I crawled along the hot, dark tunnel, and was extremely relieved to get out of there. I emerged into the daylight with a fresh insight into just how determined the Vietcong were to win the war. And they did the win the war, although it took twenty years and the loss of almost 4 million lives.

As we walked along a dirt path the sounds of distant gunfire grew louder. I thought it had been recordings to re-create the experience of war, but I realised it was live gunfire when we arrived at a shooting range.

An older guy in camouflage manning the guns suggested that the M16 had too much recoil for a girl, so I chose the AK-47. One bullet cost one US dollar. I bought five bullets and was given a pair of ear muffs.

The gun was mounted on a stand. I lent down a little, bringing the butt of the gun into contact with my shoulder. I focused on the target on the other end of the field and pulled the trigger. Five rounds rang out in quick succession, and the force of the recoil felt like being whacked in the shoulder.

'Holy shit!' I exclaimed. 'I wasn't expecting it to hurt.'

'Up until a few years ago, you could shoot a cow with a rocket launcher in Cambodia,' said a French guy who was waiting in line behind me.

I didn't know what to say to that and just shook my head dumbly and walked away. My ears were still ringing from the gunfire.

WHENEVER I RETURNED to my suite after a day spent peeling back another layer of Ho Chi Minh City, my freshly washed clothes were neatly folded on the end of my perfectly made bed. The floor was swept and the ensuite was always immaculate. Hue gave me a cold beer whenever I walked in the door, because I wasn't much of a whisky drinker. She was also a wonderful cook. Night after night she served up three or four main dishes with fluffy rice or noodles. One night we had fried frogs, which

I'd also had in Cambodia. They had plump little bottoms and bony legs that Hue dipped in egg and breadcrumbs. I wasn't much taken with frogs, but I was happy enough to eat them again.

On my last night at Les' place, Annie joined us for dinner. Les held out a dish and asked if I would like seconds.

'Mmm, yes please,' I said. 'That one is delicious. What kind of meat is it?'

'It's dog,' replied Les.

'Huh?' I said.

'I said it was dog meat.'

'You're kidding me.'

'I am not kidding, Jess. This is Vietnam. People eat dog here.'

I sat there in stunned silence. I loved dogs. Les continued talking to Annie as I sat there clasping my napkin while what Les had said sank in. A full five minutes later, he turned to me and started laughing.

'Gotcha, Mudditt,' Les said with a mischievous grin. 'It was beef.'

A security guard in Phnom Penh, Cambodia.

Dario (left), Jess and Justin at Angkor Wat in Cambodia.

Team Laos scores another goal against Team Euro (that's me to the left of the tree).

Irish Joe after getting a water buffalo on a barge in Don Set, Laos.

A night of Laos Laos shots with backpackers on Don Det, Laos.

Tom and Jess: drunk ghosts

In a monks' dormitory in Vientiane, Laos

The Banana Pancake Gang

A street hawker in Hanoi, Vietnam.

A man and his family in Ho Chi Minh City.

Les Matheson and Jess in Ho Chi Minh City, Vietnam.

Romi and Paula on that ill-fated day in Nha Trang, Vietnam.

Bad backpackers - Jess, Adam and Romi.

Bich and her sister in Hoi An.

A balancing act with a backpack

Shooting an AK-47 at the Cu Chi Tunnels in Vietnam.

13

THE MAN

After arriving back in Hanoi, I submitted my one-month tourist visa application to the Chinese embassy and spent a few wistful last days in Vietnam. Over the past three months, I had grown deeply fond of Southeast Asia and was sad to be leaving it behind. At the same time, I was wildly excited to experience China. As the giant of the region, it was a country I'd heard about on the news a million times before, yet it also had an alluring mystique.

Unfortunately, I woke up with a cold on the morning I was due to enter China. I would have rolled over and stayed under the covers, but I had already bought my bus ticket to the border crossing known as Friendship Pass. There was nothing to do but swallow a couple of paracetamol and head out to the bus station.

Once there I took one of the few remaining seats near the front of the minibus. My backpack was plonked beside me on the floor of the aisle, which was crammed with other bags and belongings.

I spent the first part of the three-hour journey trying to memorise the steps involved in getting to Nanning, which was the capital of southern Guangxi province. My head was so foggy from the cold it was a struggle to make the information stick.

'The only place in Guangxi where foreigners can cross is the Friendship Pass, known as Hue Nghi Quann in Vietnamese and Youyi Guan in Chinese,' stated my *China* Lonely Planet.

Youyi Guan, Youyi Guan, I mouthed silently, before sneezing again. I forgot the name as soon as it was out of my mouth.

Once through customs, I would need to find transport to the nearest town of Pingxiang, and then take a bus or train to Nanning, which was another four hours away. I hoped I could manage it all by nightfall.

At some point over the next couple of weeks, I would need to decide where I would go after China, and begin heading in that general direction. I scanned the list of bordering nations and thought how thrilling it was to be in a new region of the world. From China I could cross into Kazakhstan, Kyrgyzstan, Mongolia, Myanmar, Nepal, North Korea, Pakistan, Russia or Tajikistan.

Wow – North Korea. What would that be like?

The man sitting opposite me caught my eye. He pointed to the weeping blister on my lower leg. I'd burned my calf on a motorbike exhaust the day before, and had been cross with myself for being so careless. I should have known better after a month of mounting and dismounting motorbikes in Vietnam.

'Motorbike,' I said.

The man nodded sympathetically. 'China?' he asked me.

I sneezed and nodded, and we exchanged a smile. Perhaps he was surprised to see a backpacker among the dozen or so passengers.

Of the three official land border crossings between Vietnam and China, I had chosen Friendship Pass because my guidebook said it was the busiest. I had assumed this meant it was also the easiest, with the most readily available transport links to Nanning, which was itself a transport hub for onward travel. But

I had no idea whether backpackers routinely used it, and when I turned back to my guidebook I realised with a sinking feeling that I had made a mistake in choosing to travel to the border by bus. I probably should have taken the train. My guidebook said that I would need to flag a motorbike to Pingxiang because there were no bus links, and that it could be a bit of a hassle.

The oversight wasn't entirely my fault. Up until the day before I had been relying on the information provided in Lonely Planet's *Vietnam*, which hadn't flagged this as an issue. But it was a note to self for future border crossings to always check what the guidebooks said in the one for the country I was leaving behind, as well as the one I was about to enter.

I closed the book and stared out at the rugged limestone cliffs, which were soaked a deep shade of grey from the steady drizzle.

Well it's too late now to change my plans. I'll just have to wing it.

By the time we all filed off the bus, my head was so stuffed up I almost felt as if I was underwater. My limbs felt achy and my throat hurt. I swallowed another couple of paracetamol.

Our straggly group made its way along a gravel path towards an imposing classical archway in the distance, which presumably marked the beginning of Chinese territory. As I grew closer, the incline of the hill made the gate loom even larger. Across the middle were bold black Chinese characters on a red background. Its gables sloped upwards and were adorned with intricate patterns. I felt like a real adventurer as I strode under it.

The customs building was brimming with officials, traders and immigrants. I took my place in a long line and noticed that the man who had asked me about my injured leg was behind me. He carried nothing more than a black briefcase. He was middle-aged and slim, and parted his hair to one side. The line was scarcely moving, so after standing there for a couple of minutes I took off my backpack and rested it on my foot, so that I would sense right away if someone tried to grab it. Shortly after, the man from the bus pointed to an official sitting at a desk on the other side of the room. I wasn't sure what he meant, which I must have made clear by my expression. He pointed to me again, and then to the official.

'Oh right,' I said, wiping my nose. 'Should I go there?'

The man nodded and looked at me with a little frown of concern. I didn't protest when he picked up my backpack. He came over to the desk with me and looked on as my passport was duly stamped and signed. We passed through the next section together and then he indicated where I needed to stand for another passport check, and to provide my passport photos. He then ducked back to the original line.

I went outside to wait for the man so I could thank him for his help. However, I wasn't sure what language he spoke. Was he Vietnamese or Chinese? If he was Chinese, did he speak the local dialect of Cantonese or the national language of Mandarin? I'd learned Mandarin in high school, so I knew that 'xie xie' meant 'thank you', but if he spoke Cantonese, was it impolite to speak to him in Mandarin?

While waiting for the man to appear out of the sliding glass doors, I took my first proper look at China. A few sparrows hopped about on the wet grass, looking for bugs. The shrubs, trees and soil were the same muted shades of green and brown as those in my home state of Victoria. I hadn't expected China to look downright familiar.

I was first struck by the similarities of earth's topography six years earlier. I had just arrived in Morocco by ferry from Spain, and I took a bus inland to Fez. I had assumed the continent of Africa would look dramatically different from anything I'd ever seen in my life. And yet it didn't. It reminded me of my home. I had realised then that it was often the manmade parts of a nation, such as its architecture, language and dress, that lent it a distinct or exotic look.

I grinned as the man reappeared.

'Thank you,' I said in English, still holding my passport.

He smiled and nodded. I was glad he knew I was grateful for his help.

We fell into step and headed towards a couple of parked cars. The man exchanged a few words with a driver – presumably in Cantonese – who seemed to have been waiting for the man while he stood smoking a cigarette in a baggy pinstriped shirt. The man put my backpack in the boot and motioned for me to hop into the backseat. He began chatting to the driver as we sped off along the gravel road. It was raining heavily and I was relieved to have avoided the need to negotiate my own motorbike or cab fare to Pingxiang, which was about ten kilometres away.

When we were dropped off at a street corner in the sprawling metropolis, the man refused to let me pay my share. I expected that we were about to say our goodbyes, but he smiled and indicated that I should follow him. We headed over to the nearby bus station, where the man purchased two tickets and paid for my backpack to be held in a nearby storage facility. I was delighted to have sailed through the next steps in my journey and happily trotted after him along a footpath until we reached a restaurant. The man held the door open for me, and just as I was about to enter I came face-to-face with a pair of severed bear paws. They were displayed on hooks and were as big as my hands. The paws had been cooked, with the claws left intact.

I was still reeling from the macabre sight as two bowls of clear soup appeared on our table. The no-frills eatery had posters on the wall advertising soda drinks and ice creams, and it was empty except for another table of two men. Because of this, in between bringing out a pork and chicken dish, and a whole fish, the waitress hovered near us in case we needed something. I felt self-conscious using chopsticks as I found them a bit unwieldy. Most of all, I was greatly relieved not to be served bear paws.

The man and I sat in comfortable silence, although I noticed the other patrons were staring at me. I thought I'd have a sip of green tea. When the man waved his little pinkie up at me, I raised my little pinkie as I drank the tea, as though I were very posh.

Then he and the waitress laughed, poured the tea into our soup bowls, and then tipped it onto a silver tray on the table. It seemed that the tea was used to wash the bowls in between courses – but then we also drank the tea at the end of the meal. I was confused.

The waitress brought over a large bottle and set down a couple of shot glasses. The clear liquor was like some kind of liquorice firewater that burned the back of my throat. It gave me a much-needed burst of energy as we headed back to the bus station.

But first we called into a pharmacy. The man spoke to a pharmacist, who went up a step ladder and scooped out a handful of dried fungi from one of the inbuilt drawers in the wall. He bagged the mushrooms and passed them to me, along with a strip of pink tablets. The man bought me a water bottle along with the medications. I swallowed a couple of the pills right away.

For the past two hours I hadn't spent a single note of the yuan sitting in my wallet. The man had insisted on paying for everything. He also insisted on giving me his jacket to wear as I sat snivelling next to him on the bus. The air was frigid from the air conditioning, so I gratefully accepted the extra layer of warmth.

The journey to Nanning took four hours. When we got off, the man walked with me to two Western guys who had been on the same bus. They seemed a little surprised when the man tapped one of them on the shoulder and smiled and gestured towards me. I introduced myself and asked if I could go with them to find a hostel. They agreed, and told me they were from Belgium.

I gave the man back his jacket. This was goodbye. He had found me new travel companions.

'Bye-bye,' he said with a smile and a wave.

Within seconds, he had disappeared into the sea of people.

'Who was that?' one of the guys asked me.

'A very kind man,' was all I could say.

14

LONELY PLANET

I wasn't sure how the dried fungi from the pharmacy was supposed to be administered, so it was still in the brown paper bag. However, the pink tablets seemed to be working well because I woke up the next day feeling significantly better. I was excited to spend my first day sightseeing in China, and was looking forward to swapping notes with the Belgian guys over dinner.

But first, I needed a shower. I bundled up my toiletries, microfibre towel and fresh clothes, and headed off for a wash. Facilitating a trip to the shared bathroom facilities was unusually complicated. For reasons that weren't clear to me, I'd been given a laminated card rather than a key at check-in. This meant that each time I left my room, I needed the receptionist to let me back into it. The bathroom and reception were at opposite ends of a long, echoey corridor, so the back-and-forth took several minutes. It had certainly made me think twice the night before about whether I really needed to use the toilet.

The shower block was dimly lit and there was a strong smell of cleaning chemicals that reminded me of a hospital. No one else was using the facilities. In fact, the emptiness throughout the hotel was a little eerie. Finally, with wet hair and a growling stomach, I headed out onto the neat streets of Nanning to find some breakfast.

The first restaurant I entered was deserted and the waitress looked stunned to see me. She paused for a beat and then began to speak in rapid-fire Mandarin – or was it Cantonese? I had no idea.

'I don't speak Chinese,' I said.

She continued talking, and was pointing behind us to the chef's kitchen. I thought maybe the restaurant wasn't open yet.

'Sorry, I don't understand what you're saying,' I said.

I was just about to whip out my Cantonese phrasebook when two other waitresses came over to try to help. Now there were three people speaking Chinese at the same time. I felt myself blushing, and without feeling confident that I could move the conversation forward, I mumbled an apology and headed back out the door.

I walked for a few minutes before spotting a busy, cafeteria-style eatery across the road. I waited at the traffic lights with other pedestrians until the little green man began to flash. It had been ages since I'd done that. I noticed that the cars and motorbikes were parked in neat rows beside freshly cut verges. This was much tamer than Hanoi. I was excited and also a bit overwhelmed by all the Chinese characters everywhere. There seemed to be signs plastered across every flat surface. Was there this much writing in English-speaking cities? Maybe it was just because the language was indecipherable to me that I noticed it more. In Vietnam there was always at least a sprinkling of English on the signage, and Vietnamese was written in the Roman alphabet, so the foreignness of the language had just been another fun reminder that I was in a different country, rather than completely incomprehensible.

I walked into the restaurant and hovered near the door until a waitress approached me, then I pointed to the bowl of dumplings a young guy was eating at a nearby table. I rubbed my stomach and pointed at the dish again. The waitress nodded and went away, and within a couple of minutes a bowl of dumplings arrived on my table. I was pleased to have found a workaround and devoured every delicious mouthful.

I walked a few blocks to the bus station. The signs on the bus stops and the buses themselves were of course in Chinese, but Roman numerals were used for the route numbers. I found what I thought was the right bus to take me to the medicinal gardens on the city's outskirts. When I got on, I opened my guidebook and showed the driver the listing for the gardens, which had Chinese characters beside the English-language description. He nodded. I paid him two yuan and sat behind him so he could tell me when it was time to get off. The gardens were thirty minutes away, so I hoped he didn't forget I was there.

The exchange rate in China was so different from Vietnam, where one American dollar was equal to around 23,000 dong. Here, an American dollar was pegged at six yuan. That made it easier for the purposes of conversion, while also indicating that China was a much wealthier country. I'd need to be careful to ensure that my savings of Australian dollars went as far as possible.

The bus made its way through the heavy but orderly traffic, passing endless rows of identical apartment blocks under a blanket of grey sky. The only pop of colour was from billboards. At a red light, I watched a woman hang up men's business shirts on a washing line strung across her tiny balcony. I looked up at the rest of the building, where each boxy balcony represented someone's home. We were tiny specks in a sea of humanity.

Nanning had a population of 7 million, which made it bigger than any city in Australia, but I had never even heard of it until a few days ago. Apparently it wasn't popular with either domestic or foreign tourists. Those who did visit were generally using it as a gateway to Vietnam. With a population of over a billion people, China has countless massive cities like Nanning that are virtually unknown to the rest of the world.

The gardens were pleasant, if a little dry, however there was no English on the plaques so I wasn't sure what I was looking at. I wandered around a bit aimlessly and stopped to look at a group of deer lying in a dusty enclosure. A family came by with two little girls in frilly dresses and knee-high socks. Their pretty eyes widened when they saw me, but they didn't say anything.

I enjoyed a small sense of achievement at the toilet blocks when I strode confidently into those marked for females. The Chinese character for 'woman' was easy to remember because it looks like a woman crossing her legs. I wondered how I'd go when facilities weren't so clearly marked and I'd have to use sign language to ask someone where the closest toilet was.

I had learned Mandarin at school for three years, but the only character I could remember was 'zhong', because it too was self-explanatory. 'Zhong' meant 'middle' and the character consisted of a rectangle with a line through the middle. I had fond memories of dipping a calligraphy brush into a pot of ink to practise writing Mandarin characters, but learning the actual language was super hard and I quit as soon as it became an elective. Now that I was on my own in Nanning, I was regretting my lack of persistence. Or was everything in Guangxi province in Cantonese anyway? Either way, I had no clue.

I'D BEEN LOOKING FORWARD to seeing the Belgian guys, but dinner was a disappointment. They didn't drink beer and they were a bit sarcastic and cynical. By the time our meals had arrived the conversation had faltered and I quietly practised my chopstick skills when they switched to Dutch. When we had finished eating they politely wished me well and said goodbye.

I spent the next morning going up and down the escalators at Nanning Department Store. My guidebook said that China's Telecom Café was on the fifth level of the building. I had memorised the characters for 'internet café' but could not for the life of me find it.

'Wangba?' I asked a sales assistant.

She stared at me and shook her head. Maybe she just didn't understand my pronunciation.

'Wangba?' I asked two young shoppers.

They giggled and covered their mouths before practically running away from me.

'Wangba?'

A mother and daughter smiled at me kindly and continued walking.

Maybe the internet café had closed down. Or maybe I was in the wrong place. Frustrated, I gave up and headed back to the streets.

I walked along the riverfront and stopped to watch a group of old men playing mahjong on a park bench. They were smoking and laughing as they sipped green tea from a thermos in between moves. A few bystanders stood around watching the game. It seemed like a relaxing way to pass the time.

I headed on to Guangxi Provincial Museum, which had an extensive Bronze Age collection and enough English on the plaques for me to learn about it. I tried to feel more enthusiastic, but ancient history left me a little meh.

I SET out the next morning determined to find an internet café. I needed to let Mum and Dad know I had safely made it into

China or they would start to worry. I walked for ages and ages around Chaoyang Square because my guidebook unhelpfully said there were internet cafes in its 'vicinity'. But, alas, I could not find a single 'wangba'.

Most of the buildings at street level were shops, so when I saw a ground-floor office I stopped and stared. There was a large meeting table, a fish tank, some colourful abstract paintings and half a dozen people with their backs to me working away on computers. It looked like an architect's office or something similar.

I took a deep breath and walked inside. I coughed a hello. The young professionals spun round on their chairs to stare at me. Using made-up sign language that consisted of me pointing at one of their computers and pretending to type, I tried to convey that I would like to check my emails.

'Just two minutes,' I added, probably uselessly.

A young woman with a cream shirt and brown skirt stood up and indicated that I could sit in her seat. I was so grateful I wanted to hug her, but I was pretty sure she already thought I was a weirdo.

I sped-read an email from Mum and Dad describing the incessant rain and a progress report on my nephew's potty training. I began typing a brief reply, but the keyboard had different function keys and it kept switching to Chinese and making unfamiliar symbols. I hit send on the email, riddled with typos, and thanked the girl profusely.

I was back on my way with a spring in my step. The language barrier was steep, but I was doing okay. The 'point and order' strategy for meals was working, insofar as it enabled me to eat. I always went to busy restaurants and chose something after a quick glance around the diners nearby. I didn't know what I was eating, but I didn't mind. I used to joke to friends that I was like a goat because there was practically no food I didn't enjoy.

My lunch that afternoon was an exception. I was presented with a bowl of brown tubes with a gluey sauce. The gristly texture of the tubes unnerved me. Were they vocal cords? I'd read in my Lonely Planet that Nanning was famous for its dog hotpot, and I was giving its 'teeming canine cuisine district' a wide berth. However, I was well aware that all sorts of animal parts were consumed in China. I ate about four mouthfuls before giving in to my squeamishness.

After lunch it took me the entire afternoon to get the right train ticket for the next day from the massive train station. While standing in yet another wrong line, I had been gaping at a Buddhist monk ahead of me who was absorbed in a book. Unlike the monks in Southeast Asia, he wore burgundy rather than orange robes. I had assumed the couple behind me were staring at the monk too, but then I realised they were staring at me. I chuckled to myself. In Nanning, I was more of a novelty than a monk.

Back in my hotel room that evening, I talked to myself as I packed my bag. It was something I'd always been prone to, but I knew on this occasion I was listening to the sound of my voice in the hope it would make me feel less lonely. I hadn't spoken to a single person for three days. In Southeast Asia there had always been someone around who spoke a bit of English. In China, so far, the lack of English was absolute. Hawkers didn't even really try to sell me stuff – I guess a foreigner like me was in the too-hard basket.

You're in China. Everyone speaks Chinese. What did you expect?

I folded my t-shirts into squares and placed them inside my backpack. I laid out my clothes to save me time in the morning and then zipped up my bag. I sat on the end of the bed and stared forlornly out the window at the skyscrapers lit up against the night sky.

I thought I'd been ready to challenge myself as a backpacker, but I had bitten off more than I could chew in China. I wasn't really getting any value out of the experience because I didn't understand what was going on around me. I couldn't honestly say I was enjoying myself. Had it been a mistake to come?

Maybe I'd have an easier time in Yangshuo, where I was headed in the morning. It was meant to have beautiful scenery and was one of Guangxi provinces most popular tourist destinations, so perhaps I'd meet other English speakers there. I just had to make sure I got on the right train.

I sighed. If I did decide it had been a mistake to come to China, it would take me at least a week to travel across its vast territory to cross into another country. I might be lonely for a while.

15

MY GOOD FORTUNE

I was savouring a cup of coffee in a cute café in Yangshuo when two backpackers wandered in and took a seat at the table across from me. The guy had shaggy blond hair poking out of his beanie and the girl was very slim and wore cargo pants with a black turtleneck. I felt an instant rush of camaraderie, but I waited until they had ordered some food before catching the girl's eye and giving her a grin and a wink. I was expecting her to wave me over to their table, but she responded with a quick half nod and weak smile. Then she turned back to her boyfriend, who hadn't skipped a beat in their conversation. I don't think he had registered my presence.

Embarrassed, I stared into the bottom of my coffee cup. It was the first conversation I had heard in English for almost a week and it was painful not to be part of it. At that moment their American accents sounded like sublime choral music. I paid for my coffee and left without looking back at the girl.

We'd be best friends by now if we were in Southeast Asia, I thought as I kicked a pebble into the gutter while heading towards Li River.

At any rate, I was bound to see more backpackers. Yangshuo

was like something out of a storybook, with cobbled streets, old wooden shopfronts, and a dramatic backdrop of lush forest and tall limestone peaks. It attracted a steady stream of domestic tourists, and there were clues that a significant number of international ones came there too: the pedestrian-only thoroughfare in the centre of town was called 'Foreigner Street' and some of the menus had English on them.

I passed a row of stalls selling traditional crafts like silk jackets and scroll paintings. I stopped to browse a rack of chiffon scarves and pulled out a red-and-black one with a geometric pattern. A hawker materialised out of nowhere.

'How much?' I asked her.

She pointed at the sign above the rack.

'One hundred yuan?' I exclaimed, aghast. I shook my head and put the scarf back. The nights were chilly in Yangshuo and I needed a scarf. However, getting the hawker down from such a high starting price would be a lot of work with my limited language skills, and I wasn't in the right frame of mind to do battle.

I HAD RECENTLY ENJOYED a memoir called *American Shaolin*, which was about a guy called Matthew Polly who spent two years studying kung fu with monks in China. When I saw a brochure at my hotel advertising lessons, I metaphorically leaped at the chance.

The class was held in an open-air shed on top of a hill. The roof was supported by bamboo pillars, which were likely felled from the forest of bamboo that grew along the side. After warming up with a few stretches and a pep talk about the importance of focus and strength, the kung-fu master leaped through the air like a jungle cat and landed softly on his feet.

'I don't think I can do that,' I said dubiously. 'I don't have proper shoes, either.'

'You will try. A positive mindset is important to the study of kung fu,' he reminded me.

'Right,' I said. 'I will leap through the air.'

But within twenty minutes my thigh muscles were trembling from fatigue and I was covered in sweat. I could lift myself off the ground, but I came back down with the thud of a baby elephant. I looked at my watch again. A two-hour class was going to test my endurance.

Perhaps I should have tried tai chi instead.

The guy and girl on the other side of the shed looked as if they were having fun learning a series of gentle movements. Their teacher was dressed in flowing white robes and seemed to ooze serenity. My guy was compact and muscly, and wore shorts, trainers and a t-shirt.

'Move your foot further back. Yes – but keep your balance,' said Master Liu, turning back to me as I wobbled and gritted my teeth.

I tried to copy the next position he adopted. Right leg extended back in a lunge. Drop the knee. Left hand on hip. Right arm out straight, palm upturned. I focused my gaze on a clump of bamboo as I held the position. It was deeply uncomfortable.

I was about halfway through the lesson when the girl came over and asked if I could take a few action shots of them with their teacher. I happily obliged, and was relieved to get a few minutes' rest. We had a quick chat and they told me they were graphic designers from Manchester. Joanna and Chris had been on the road for almost four months, as I had.

When our respective classes ended, I decided not to risk embarrassing myself by asking if they wanted to meet up for drinks or a meal later. Instead, I just smiled and wished them well on their travels.

'You too, Jess. Lovely meeting you,' Joanna said.

She and Chris wandered off down the gravel path holding hands and chatting happily.

I thanked Master Liu for the class and expressed my admiration for his mastery of such an intense martial art. Then I drank almost a whole litre of water and headed back to my guesthouse with my head held high.

I WOKE up the next morning feeling as though I'd pulled every muscle in my body. Even lifting my arm to brush my teeth was painful. As I hopped onto a creaky mountain bike, I hoped the guided bicycle tour through the countryside would ease the stiffness rather than make it worse.

The group of four I was in set off over one of Yangshuo's many arched bridges, beneath which was a pond filled with pink water lilies. Soon the sealed road had turned into a dirt track and our female guide led us past verdant rice paddies and a farmyard filled with ducks, geese and chickens. A man in gumboots carried a bucket towards a stall of black pigs, who were noisily awaiting their slops.

When we stopped to take photos of a lake where water buffalo bathed, I didn't approach the two other travellers on the tour. I think they were Chinese-Americans, but I didn't launch into my usual volley of questions to find out. We each took different vantage points to photograph the vista. After a few minutes, we hopped back on our bikes and continued along the track in single file.

I thought about how different the vibe was from backpackers

in China compared with Southeast Asia. There was no expectation that we would hang out just because we happened to be in the same country at the same time. Getting off the so-called Banana Pancake Trail had been quite a shock, but I was beginning to see the upsides. Some backpackers were kind of annoying, and they were often the ones who were keenest to pair up. Plus, I loved solitude most of the time. It was one of the reasons why I had wanted to travel solo in the first place. Being alone made it possible to fully absorb my surroundings because I wasn't distracted by chitchat. Perhaps all I needed was a few fleeting encounters every now and again. I would have loved to have seen Tom from Laos while I was in China, but he had emailed me back to say that he was staying in Taiwan for the next couple of weeks. Ah well.

I pedalled on happily, content in my thoughts. The air was crisp, the sun was on my back and the scenery was achingly beautiful.

I WAS STANDING on a bridge in Guilin when a young woman came up to me holding a camera. Smiling, she pointed at me and then back at the camera. I smiled and nodded in agreement. We stood beside each other as her husband took a few snaps of us with a temple on the lake behind us.

I felt like a giant next to this woman – she was in heels, yet still only came up to my shoulder. Our differences didn't stop there. She wore a pale-pink dress with a short-sleeved cardigan studded with rhinestones, while I was in Velcro-strapped Teva sandals, fisherman pants and a yellow singlet. My accessories were a dog-tag necklace and a black leather baseball cap. The woman beamed and said something in Chinese as she clasped my hand and gave a little bow. I smiled and they were gone.

As soon as I'd arrived in Guilin the day before, I'd been

struck by how much attention I was getting. People would smile and point at me, and I'd been in about five photos in less than twenty-four hours. Backpackers tended to flock to nearby Yangshuo, while Guilin was hugely popular with domestic tourists, who were clearly in a carefree mood and had time to stop and have a photo with a big daggy giraffe.

When a girl approached me about ten minutes later, I assumed she was going to ask for a photo too. I almost fell over when she started speaking to me in English.

'Hi! My name is Mei-Xing,' she said. 'I am an engineering student at Guilin University.'

'Nice to meet you, Mei-Xing,' I said. 'I'm Jess from Australia.'

'I have finished my classes for today. Would you like me to show you around the city?'

'I would love that,' I replied. 'That's really kind of you.'

'It will be my pleasure,' she said. 'I am happy to have the chance to practise my English. It's not very good. I'm sorry for that.'

'Your English is excellent,' I said, beaming. 'My Chinese is terrible.'

Mei-Xing laughed. Like me, she had a sporty kind of look, and was wearing parachute material tracksuit pants, trainers and a polo-neck t-shirt. However, Mei-Xing was dressed from head to toe in white, whereas I never bought anything white because I couldn't keep it clean.

We jumped on a bus and headed towards the city's largest park. Mei-Xing told me its name was Qīxīng Gōngyuán, which meant 'Seven Star Park.' When viewed from above, its seven karst peaks resembled the shape of the Big Dipper constellation.

We joined the throngs of other visitors and walked up a bitumen trail to a viewing platform with a sweeping view of the parklands below, which were dotted with several imposing Buddhist temples, pavilions and a bonsai garden. Parts of it had a theme-park feel. We walked along a platform through a cave filled with stalagmites and lit up in a rainbow kaleidoscope of floodlights, with boppy Chinese pop playing over loudspeakers.

Near a refreshments and souvenir stall was a man and a woman dressed in traditional garb of red satin robes and huge, floppy hats. Nearby, a man held a monkey on a leash that was dressed like a baby in a onesie. An older man passed him some cash to have a photo with the monkey and his wife. Mei-Xing took some photos of me sitting in a swing chair with peacocks perched either side.

Next we came to a small zoo.

'Ooh pandas!' I cried. 'They are so adorable. Look at that little one munching on bamboo leaves.' I felt so happy to have seen pandas in China. The cage was really small though.

We were standing next to a camel adorned with decorative tassels when a mother and her tween daughter asked me for a photo. I once again towered over the women, who were both in pretty dresses. We all smiled and made a V sign with our right hand, which I had become accustomed to doing in photos.

Mei-Xing took yet more photos of me as I stood in the spot where former American President Bill Clinton had given a speech in 1998. The plaque said he was there for an environment protection forum. It was very convenient to be able to ask Mei-Xing to take a photo of me, rather than putting the request to a passer-by using sign language. I tended only to do that when I really, really wanted a photo with me in a particular spot.

We came to a bridge that was supported by four brick arches in the shape of semi-circles. The reflection of the arches in the water created full circles and the effect was almost an optical illusion, making it appear as if there were tunnels of water. Near the bridge was a grand weeping willow, whose tendrils grazed the assortment of white and mauve water lilies. The scene reminded me of a Monet painting.

'This is Flower Bridge,' said Mei-Xing. 'It's a thousand years old.'

'It's very beautiful,' I said, kneeling down to better capture it in a photo.

Reflections were used to great effect in Chinese architecture, and I was awed by how ancient some of it was. In Australia a building was considered old if it had been constructed more than a century ago. In China, evidence of past dynasties went back millennia.

It was quite late in the afternoon by then, but Mei-Xing offered to show me around her campus, so we jumped back on a bus and headed to Guilin University of Electronic Technology. Its expansive grounds contained apartment-block style buildings for lectures and student dormitories, plus a large manmade lake. It was leafy and well-maintained, and dramatic limestone cliffs made for an attractive backdrop.

We were walking along a path when we came to two men sitting in front of a laminated sign. One of the men looked very old and wore dark glasses. His left arm was missing from the elbow.

'This is a famous fortune teller in Guilin. He is blind, but it is said that he can see into the future. Would you like to have your fortune told? It's ten yuan.'

'I'd love to,' I said. 'I've never had my fortune told before. But please ask him not to tell me when he thinks I will die.'

'Okay, sure.'

The man took my right hand and gently squeezed it. Then he turned my palm over and moved his thumb in light strokes across it.

'The fortune teller speaks a local dialect that I don't understand, so his assistant will translate what he says into what we call "city-Cantonese",' explained Mei-Xing.

The fortune teller's assistant asked Mei-Xing for my date of birth and the time I was born. She then told the assistant what I had said. The assistant told the fortune teller.

The fortune teller thought for a few moments, then spoke to his assistant. The assistant relayed to Mei-Xing what he had said, and then she told me.

'The fortune teller senses that you feel sorry for poor people,' said Mei-Xing.

'Yes, I do,' I said, nodding slowly. 'Although I think most people do.'

The fortune teller spoke again. He was still holding my hand.

'He also says that you will become a professor.'

Given that I was on university grounds, that seemed a fairly safe prediction. However, I actually had been thinking about doing a PhD – although I had no idea what I would do it on. Perhaps I needed to give it some more thought.

'He says that you will have two daughters.'

'I would love that,' I said.

'And that you will be wealthy, although not until you're in your fifties.'

'I guess I can wait,' I replied with a laugh.

We thanked the fortune teller and kept going. It was starting to get dark. We came to an area lit with floodlights and half a dozen table tennis tables. Every table had a match in play. Table tennis was to China what cricket was to Australia – immensely popular. Mei-Xing told me it was her country's national sport. The regular competitions were held on the weekends – these were just social matches, she said. We took a seat on a park bench to watch.

'I love table tennis,' I said. 'I used to play with my dad all the time. We had a table tennis table in our garage.'

'Do you want to play?' asked Mei-Xing.

'I'd love to!' I said. 'Let's have a game.'

'Oh, I'm not good at table tennis,' she replied. 'I'll go ask one of those guys.'

One of the players graciously gave up his bat and I began a warm-up volley with the other guy. Mei-Xing cheered me on and kept score in both languages. She jokingly referred to it as an international match between China and 'Aodàlìyǎ', which was how 'Australia' was pronounced. I did my best to return my opponent's lightning-fast serves, but I was squarely defeated. Grinning and sweaty, we shook hands.

I flopped into bed that night with a big smile on my face. It had been my best day yet in China.

OVER THE NEXT couple of days Mei-Xing showed me many of the city's popular spots, such as a strip that was famous for delicious street snacks, a shopping district and another couple of parks. As well as relieving me of the need to have my head permanently stuffed in a map and translating menus, Mei-Xing showed me how to buy a bottle of shampoo from a supermarket, where things were cheaper. We took a laminated card to the counter and exchanged it for the bottle of shampoo after handing over the cash. I asked Mei-Xing about the card I had been given instead of a key at the hotel in Nanning.

'I think you probably needed to pay a deposit in order to be given the key,' she said. 'That is quite common at hotels.'

'Ooh,' I said. 'That makes sense. I guess they weren't able to explain that to me.'

It was also great to be able to ask Mei-Xing about local customs – I liked to test whether what I had read in my Lonely Planet stacked up with a local. While dipping beef strips into the broth of a hotpot one night, I asked Mei-Xing if she ate dog meat.

'I've never had it,' she said. 'It's expensive. It's something that is eaten on special occasions or if you're wealthy and can afford it.'

Mei-Xing told me her family was poor. She had grown up in a village a few hundred kilometres from Guilin and she was the only child of subsistence farm labourers. A few years ago, her father had begun working as a barber because the money was better. In order to pay for one year of her university tuition fees, he needed to give 4000 haircuts.

Mei-Xing worked really hard to make her father's investment in her worthwhile. After dropping me on the doorstop of my hotel at night, she took the bus back to campus and would study until midnight. She would be up again by six or seven in the morning to study before breakfast. My year of backpacking was so decadent by comparison.

Mei-Xing told me she had never seen a foreigner until a couple of years ago, after she had moved to Guilin. She had been excited to see a foreign girl wandering around the city, because she didn't get many opportunities to practise speaking English. But she had been nervous about whether I would agree to hang out with her.

'I can't tell you how glad I was to meet you!' I said. 'I'd been quite lonely. You're the first person I've met in China who speaks English so well. How did you learn so quickly?'

'I just enjoy studying it in my spare time,' she said shyly.

I told Mei-Xing that it was very lucky for me that she had such an interest in English. I don't know what I would have done if I didn't have the good fortune to meet her.

MEI-XING ACCOMPANIED me to the bus station on the morning I was headed to Guangzhou, which is the capital of Guangdong province and was previously known as Canton. Just before I boarded the bus, she gave me a keyring with a photo of Guilin's cityscape.

'Thank you for making Guilin a highlight of my time in China,' I said. 'I wish you all the best for the rest of your studies.'

'It's been my pleasure, Jess. I am happy to have a friend from Australia,' she said.

We gave each other a big hug and she waved goodbye until the bus pulled out of the dock.

I was feeling a little flat, so I was over the moon when the bus driver put on a Mr Bean film. It was nice to be able to laugh when my fellow passengers laughed – for once we were all in on the same joke. It made sense that the non-verbal Mr Bean was popular in China – his humour was universal and did not rely on subtitles. As I watched his bumbling antics, it dawned on me that I resembled Mr Bean in China. I laughed to myself – it was actually pretty funny.

Unfortunately, the loneliness hit me hard in Guangzhou. I felt a bit bereft without Mei-Xing. It was raining when I got off the bus and I had serious trouble finding a hotel. I couldn't even find a taxi, as the cars whizzed past me without any designated area to stop. I must have looked a sight for sore eyes on the footpath because a businessman approached me and walked me to the other side of the street, where he phoned a hotel on his mobile phone while holding his umbrella over us. Then he hailed me a cab and told the driver where to go. I was so grateful to him. I took extra copies of the hotel's business card at the check-in desk and put one in each of my bags and trouser pockets, as I didn't know where I was on the map.

My hotel room was accessed via two flights of downward steps from reception – it was like an underground bunker. It was deathly cold and obviously windowless. I immediately switched on the TV and had the state-run broadcaster, CCTV, playing in the background just for comfort. The silence had been overwhelming.

The next morning I tried and failed to find the Temple of the Six Banyan Trees and the Temple of the Five Immortals, so I went to a market and saw thousands of exotic animals squirming about in small cages. Guangzhou was a concrete jungle, with endless flyovers and ring roads, skyscrapers and malls. I got on the wrong bus and it was ages before the next stop gave me a chance to get off and retrace my steps.

My second day was no better as I spent half of it hopelessly lost while looking for the regional bus station. As I grumpily stomped up and down the same street four times while looking for a road I simply couldn't find, I thought what a waste of time it all was. If I was in Southeast Asia, my guesthouse would simply have arranged my onward travel.

When I did find the bus station, I decided to cut my losses and leave Guangzhou the next morning. With the precious ticket in my hand, my mood immediately brightened. By this time tomorrow, I'd be at my cousin's house in Hong Kong. Philip was a lawyer and heaps of fun. His wife, Anne, was Irish, and they had two little kids called Jack and Bella. I'd met Anne years ago in London when she and Philip were dating, and she was friendly and kind.

I flicked to the page of my notebook where I'd jotted down the the address. Just seeing it brought a smile to my lips. The Reids lived at Amigo Mansion in Happy Valley. My expectations were sky high.

16

RAGS TO RICHES

I adjusted a pair of goggles over my eyes, took a deep breath and dived to the bottom of the pool. As I swam along the bottom, I used my hands to feel the smooth surface for Anne's engagement ring, which she had lost the day before.

As I cased the shallow end of the pool, it struck me that I'd gone from rags to riches in the space of twenty-four hours. The day before I'd been in my grim bunker room in Guangzhou. Today I was diving for diamonds at the exclusive Hong Kong Football Club.

Anne and Philip had sponsored my application for temporary admittance at the private members' club, which had resort-like facilities and a variety of sporting clubs. Established during the days of the British Empire, the club was encased inside the racetrack of the Happy Valley Racecourse, where millions of Hong Kong dollars were won and lost in a single night. The thick perimeter of lawn made the club feel like a green oasis in a pulsating city of skyscrapers.

Gasping for air, I came back up to the surface.

'I didn't see it, Anne,' I said.

'Me neither,' she said, her big blue eyes filled with worry.

She had turned over all the banana lounge mattresses on the pool deck.

We spent an hour trying to find the missing ring, but without any luck. Anne and I headed back to Amigo Mansion, which was just across the road. It was not an actual mansion, as its name denoted, but a collection of boutique apartments. I felt silly for having thought my cousins lived in a free-standing house – I don't think there is such a thing in Hong Kong. It was a sunlit apartment with the most incredible view of the racecourse and skyline.

Jack and Bella (as they called her for short) had just woken from their nap and their nanny, Ritaly, was giving them some chopped fruit and cheese sticks. I gave Bella a toy puppy I'd bought from a street hawker in Guangzhou. She giggled when it gave a mechanical yip and wagged its tail, and her whole face lit up with delight. She had the most beautiful blonde curls. Her big brother was stomping around with a green truck and a bucket of Lego. Anne told him not to tip it out on the floor, which he promptly did with a mischievous grin that reminded me of his dad.

We headed back out and walked to a small park with a playground. There were a few other expat kids already there, with their nannies standing close by and chatting away like old friends. Ritaly went over to say hello to them. As Anne and I pushed Jack and Bella on the swings, she told me most of their expat friends had Filipino nannies. English was an official language of the Philippines, so communicating with a Filipino nanny was easy.

I told Anne how I'd spent much of the past couple of weeks being totally lost and confused. I started laughing as I told her how I'd walk into a restaurant and point to another diner's meal because I couldn't read the menus, and how kind strangers would try to help me when they saw how clueless I was.

The language barrier had been lifted from the moment I passed through customs at the special economic zone of Shenzen. Being able to read Hong Kong's bilingual street signs was a revelation and I did a double take when I saw British place names like Aberdeen and Queens Road. I felt as if I'd entered another country – which I basically had. The stamp in my passport stated I had left Chinese territory, and having a multiple-entry Chinese visa meant I could return.

Hong Kong had been handed back from the British in 1997 after one hundred and fifty-six years of colonial rule. But it had not been absorbed back into China holus-bolus. It was deemed a 'special administrative region', which meant it had separate economic and political systems. The biggest difference was that Hong Kong's citizens voted in regular elections, whereas China was a one-party state.

'On my way to your place yesterday I took a red double-decker tram – and I saw a sign to a place called Soho!' I exclaimed to Anne. 'And I'm getting used to cars driving on the left side of the road again. It's like being in London,' I said.

'Well, except for the weather,' Anne replied wistfully, giving Bella a big push. 'I think it's more the humidity than the heat that I struggle with. After six years here, I can't tell you how much I long to be wrapped up in a blanket in front of a roaring fire, drinking a cup of tea.'

'I'm kind of the opposite,' I replied. 'I'm so happy to be missing Melbourne's freezing winter. I feel so lucky to get an entire year of summer temperatures on my trip.'

'You're going to have an amazing tan by the end of it,' said Anne, whose complexion was porcelain white with a sprinkling of freckles. 'Your parents won't recognise you when you meet up with them in London next year.'

'They won't,' I agreed.

I knew it wasn't just my tan that would make me seem different. I loved my new life on the road and I didn't want to give it up. The prospect of returning to a nine-to-five job, even in an exciting city like London, filled me with dread. I pushed the thought away, as I still had another eight months left before I had to face it.

WHEN PHILIP GOT HOME from work, we caught up over a beer on the balcony. We were reminiscing about the big family Christmases we'd have in Melbourne when our grandparents were still alive. His family would drive down from Sydney and stay with us, and we had Easter holidays with the Reids – as we affectionally called them – in their beautiful beachside suburb of Manly in Sydney.

I said how lucky Philip was to live in Asia – and to be right across from the Hong Kong Football Club with its amazing swimming pool.

'It's pretty great,' Philip said as he cracked open a second beer. 'I've actually got Gaelic football training on that pitch on the right in half an hour. I've been playing a lot of it over the past couple of years – it's a fantastic sport.'

'How fun. Maybe I could come and watch?'

'Why don't you come train with us? It's a mixed team. And we need all the players we can get for the practice match tonight.'

'I've never played Gaelic football in my life – but sure, I'll give it a go,' I said. 'Although I haven't got any sneakers.'

'I've got a spare pair you can borrow,' said Philip.

'Okay, thanks. I'll go and get changed,' I said, immediately deciding not to finish what was left in my can of beer.

I went to my room – which was usually Jack's room – and did my best to cobble together a training outfit from the limited choices in my backpack. Philip's shoes were a bit big, so I put on my thick grey woollen socks. They came halfway up my shins. I looped a brown leather belt through the leopard print shorts I usually wore to bed as a way of keeping them up if I was tackled. My orange-and-yellow striped t-shirt had begun to sport a few moth-holes.

I laughed at my reflection in the mirror. *Ah well. It's not like anyone knows me.*

A wave of regret passed through me when Philip introduced me to his teammates – a surprising number of whom were hotties. Everyone welcomed me with big, friendly smiles, and everyone but me was in slick sports gear. I assumed they were high-flying lawyers or bankers like my cousin. I was the fifth girl out of twenty or so players.

Anyhow, that was the last time I thought about my dorky socks. We trotted out onto the well-watered turf for some warm-up exercises and I had to focus on getting my head around the rules of the game.

Gaelic football is the Irish version of soccer and Philip had described it as somewhat similar to rugby, which he also loved. The ball could be carried, bounced, kicked, hand-passed or 'soloed', which was when a player dropped the ball and kicked it back up to themselves while on the move.

After twenty minutes, we split into teams for a practice match. Philip picked me to go on his team so I donned a blue singlet.

I took up my position as a forward and a whistle was blown. The positions on the field were much like hockey, so it was easy enough for me to understand what I was meant to do. I sprinted after the ball in hot pursuit and passed it off as strategically as I could. I tried a solo but was like a rabbit in headlights – I couldn't pull off the unfamiliar technique under pressure and completely mucked it up. The next time, I just passed it off.

When I intercepted a pass, one of the hottest guys on the team gave me a high five.

The whistle blew to signal the end of the match and the blue team cheered – we'd won. I walked off the pitch with a grin. Being part of a team again felt amazing. It was also the most magnificent setting for a sporting field I'd ever set foot on. Around one side of the six or so pitches were glittering skyscrapers, and on the other side was the pitch-black forest of Victoria Peak. Just being out there had made me feel like a superstar.

Philip and I went back to the apartment to change and pick up Anne before jumping in a cab. We were headed to an Irish pub called Delaney's in Wan Chai, where we were meeting up with some of the other players for beers.

It was a big pub, but it felt cosy, with brown leather chairs and sturdy oak tables, wooden floorboards and framed paintings all over the varnished timber-panelled walls. I couldn't see anyone in the bar of Asian descent – even the bartenders were Westerners.

Anne was recalling a funny anecdote about her day in her delightful Irish accent as Philip returned from the bar with a grin and a tray of Guinness pints.

'To my well-travelled cousin from Melbourne,' said Philip as the six of us clinked our glasses.

I wiped the froth off my lips and grinned at the familiar faces around me at the table. In that moment, I actually felt as if I was in Ireland – except, of course, that the air was crisp with air conditioning.

I caught sight of a cocktail list and reeled – a single martini was more than my daily budget. Hong Kong was wildly expensive and I most probably would have bypassed it if not for Philip and Anne's hospitality.

As the night wore on and Philip generously shouted us more rounds, the Guinness loosened my lips and I couldn't stop blabbering. I felt so happy to be understood. The other players were also Aussies and hearing the vernacular again was surreal. And yet midway through my third pint, I was suddenly struck with a strange sensation. I missed China.

THE NEXT MORNING I rode a colonial-era cable tram up the highest mountain on Hong Kong Island, Victoria Peak. The incline was so steep at one point that I felt as if I'd been strapped in to some kind of rocket ship from a bygone era.

Before the tram was introduced in 1888, colonial officers and their families used to be carried up the mountain in sedan chairs. Locals were only allowed to use the tram during off-peak times, and they were banned from building homes in the area until 1930. The entitlement took my breath away as much as the view.

At the top of the peak was a futuristic glass building that had clothing stores and a Madame Tussaud's museum. Out the front was a wax model of the city's most famous export, the movie star Jackie Chan. He was about to strike an opponent with his fists and a high kick and he wore a black-and-yellow Lycra suit. I asked another tourist to take my photo next to the kung-fu star and then followed a power walker along a path that came to a viewing platform.

From the lookout, the skyscrapers resembled a collection of sharpened pencils. Some were so tall they almost seemed to graze the cotton-wool clouds. The panorama was layered like a trifle, with forest followed by the cream and pale pink cream skyscrapers, then the waters of Victoria Harbour and yet more skyscrapers on the island of Kowloon.

'It's beautiful, isn't it?' said the guy standing beside me in a French accent.

'Yes, it's really lovely,' I replied. 'I think I've taken about forty photos.'

'Did you know that Hong Kong has more skyscrapers than anywhere else in the world?'

'I did not,' I said. 'But that doesn't surprise me.'

We got chatting. Gabriel told me he lived in Shanghai, where his fiancée was from. He had lived in China for five years and could speak Mandarin. He had come to Hong Kong for a business meeting that morning, and he liked to take a walk around the peak when he was in town.

'All the skyscrapers you can see were designed with feng shui principles. Do you know what feng shui is?'

'Not really,' I admitted.

'It's a way of harnessing the positive energy of the earth – the Chinese call it "qi".'

Gabriel went on to tell me how many of the major buildings have a clear view of the harbour, because open water is associated with prosperity and would bring success to the businesses. But when the Bank of China was built, the architects ignored feng shui principles. Its knife-like edges point at the famous HSBC building next door, and British Government House, and it also featured an 'X' which is a letter associated with death. Bad things started happening. The British governor lost his job, and then his successor had a heart attack. Hong Kong was hit by an economic downturn. People said a curse had befallen the city because of the disrespect towards feng shui practices.

'That's extraordinary,' I said. 'Is the city still cursed?'

'No, because they installed two cannons on the roof of the HSBC Building. They pointed towards the Bank of China to deflect the bad luck. They also put bronze lions on the ground floor to promote prosperity and harmony. It stopped the negative energy circulating.'

'Isn't it amazing that in a global financial hub like Hong

Kong, where cash is king and data is everything, its residents can adhere to an ancient superstition?'

'Yes, it's something. China itself is full of apparent contradictions. It's like an onion – with every layer you unpeel, the more interesting it becomes.'

'Mmm yes,' I said, still thinking over everything Gabriel had told me.

'I have to get going now, but it's been nice talking to you, Jess. Here – this is my email address,' he said as he passed me his business card. 'Drop me an email if you come to Shanghai and I can show you around.'

'Thanks so much, Gabriel. I'll be there for sure,' I said.

There was no doubt in my mind. I wanted to see more of this fascinating country.

∼

I AM a sucker for any kind of world record, so when I read in my guidebook that Hong Kong was home to the world's longest escalator, I made a beeline for it.

The Mid-Levels escalators were built in the 1980s to connect two parts of the city. The terrain was so steep between the affluent Mid-Levels residential district and the busy Central District near Victoria Harbour that it was impossible to build a major road. As a result, office workers were forced to commute using an alternative route and the traffic congestion was getting worse and worse.

I filed onto the escalator and stood behind a young woman in a black corporate suit and heels. It was open-air but had a roof to protect against inclement weather. The apartments opposite were like matchboxes. Most didn't have a balcony and the teeny tiny windows were covered with bars. The whole of Hong Kong is only 1100 square kilometres, and it has the fourth-highest population density in the world. I'd grown up in a country with one of the world's lowest population densities. On average, Australia has three people per square kilometre: in Hong Kong there are more than 6000 people in the same area.

Another ten minutes passed as I travelled along at a snail's pace. I tapped my fingers on the side and kept looking at the concrete jungle opposite. Feeling silly, I took a couple of photos of myself. I wanted to be able to say I had ridden the world's longest escalator the whole eight hundred metres and travelled up the equivalent of forty-five floors, but I decided to get off about halfway at Tai Kwun. I wanted to explore Hollywood Road, which was known for its antique stores and art galleries. It was also one of the first roads to be paved after British colonial rule began in 1841, and the city's oldest temple was built there soon after. Man Mo Temple was dwarfed by the apartment blocks surrounding it, and it looked a bit worn and grimy. Inside was a different story. The red, black and gold decor created a sumptuous feast for the eyes. Suspended from the ceiling of the prayer hall were gigantic incense coils in the shape of an ice cream cone. Inside each coil was a sheet of red paper with black calligraphy script. I assumed these were prayers for the dearly departed. A young woman held three sticks of incense as she prayed with her eyes closed. A shaft of sunlight illuminated the fragrant smoke. There were large golden cauldrons with lions' heads. Timber lattice divided the different parts of the hall.

Once back on the street, I bought some chicken-ball skewers from a street hawker. I ate them as I walked past a row of gorgeous red-brick buildings with elegant archways. I didn't dare go inside an eating establishment in Hong Kong because the prices would be astronomical. Philip had taken me out for yum cha the day before, and it probably cost him a couple of hundred dollars. We'd gone to an upmarket restaurant called Peking Garden that was near his office and, once again, I'd felt embarrassed by what I was wearing. Everyone else had been in corporate suits and shiny leather shoes and I had on hiking sandals and denim shorts.

I was much more at ease perusing the flea market. An old man nodded at me as I approached his stall. He wore a singlet and had Coke-bottle glasses. I pored over his treasure trove of vintage cameras, porcelain plates, jade rings and ancient maps. I bought a small bronze elephant for Grandma and then posted it with some postcards that were in my bag. Then I zipped back to Amigo Mansion on the metro. Travelling in Hong Kong was a piece of cake.

ANNE HAD an appointment the next morning so we planned to meet up at the club after lunch. I flashed my membership card on the front desk and was given two fluffy pool towels. I buried my head in the softness and inhaled the freshly laundered scent.

After paddling about in the water, I sunbaked on a banana lounge while flicking through a British issue of *Grazia* Anne had lent me. I was so out of touch with celebrity news that it was like checking in from outer space.

I eavesdropped on the two women next to me who were talking about who would be attending some big fundraising lunch. One had a British accent and a big straw hat, and the other sounded American. She was wearing a fuchsia beach wrap and had frizzy blonde hair. Both were absolutely dripping in jewels and had beautifully manicured nails.

I had soon completely dried off under the hot sun, so I gathered my belongings and headed to the coffee shop, which had a view of the pool. A waiter presented me with a huge club sandwich, a side of French fries and a tall glass of Diet Coke. He asked me to sign the bill, but I didn't have to pay. Anne had told me to put my food and drinks on the family account, as cash wasn't used at the club. I signed the bill nonchalantly, as though I did stuff like that every day. I couldn't help it – my upmarket surroundings were rubbing off on me.

I browsed the library shelves and then perused the racks of merchandise at the club store before settling down to send the group email I'd compiled on my PDA back at Anne and Philip's place. I breathlessly told my 'darlings' how much fun I was having in Hong Kong, and that I was going to my third Gaelic football training session that night. I attached the photo of me riding the escalator and posing with a wax model of Jackie Chan. I signed off by saying that I was about to check out the club's sauna and steam room and would then maybe have another swim, before meeting up with Anne for a cappuccino.

Rags to riches, I murmured to myself with a smile as I hit send.

17

BRIGHT LIGHTS, BIG CITY

The train conductor pointed to the plaque on the wall to indicate that the berth number corresponded with the ticket in my hand, and then he disappeared down the aisle to help someone else.

I gazed up at the top bed of a triple bunk, which was where I'd be spending the next twenty hours. The hard sleeper carriage could hold six people, with a gap between the two sets of bunks that was only about the width of my shoulders. None of the carriages on the train had doors, which meant that anyone passing along the aisle could peer in at those who were resting on their bunks, and the noise of fifty or so passengers bounced around in what was essentially a big tin can. The upside to the lack of doors was that the space felt less confined.

A middle-aged woman sitting on the bottom bunk looked surprised to see me, then smiled and spoke to the person on the top bunk opposite mine. A young guy, who I guessed was her son, leaped down the ladder at the end of his bed and offered to hoist my backpack onto the storage rack. I gratefully passed him my pack and watched as he straddled the gap between the ladder and the rack above the aisle, then fastened one of the straps to a pole to prevent it falling off. His mother nodded approvingly and continued peeling her orange.

'Xie xie,' I said to the guy by way of a thank you.

We grinned at each other. He was about six foot two and had the build of a basketball player, with tousled hair and a chiselled jawline. He wore a plain white t-shirt with jeans.

'Wǒ láizì Aodàlìyǎ,' I ventured, which means, 'I am from Australia.'

'Aodàlìyǎ!' he said with a grin.

I nodded vigorously and kept smiling. I wondered why he was going to Shanghai, or whether he lived there.

I had no idea what he said next, so I shook my head and shrugged.

We laughed.

An elderly couple appeared at the entrance to the carriage and the young guy placed their bags next to mine with the same pleasant demeanour. His mother shuffled up the bottom bunk so they had space to sit there too.

I climbed up the ladder to my bunk. It was higher off the ground than I realised. I couldn't sit up without bumping my head on the ceiling, so I lay on my stomach as I rummaged around in my day bag for my book and water bottle. The young guy was back in his bunk now. We smiled at one another from our opposite beds.

What a dreamboat. If only we could communicate.

The train pulled out of the busy station with a lurch and I rolled against the steel railing that served as protection between me and the ground below. The train quickly picked up speed and we whizzed past endless apartment blocks before the carriage was plunged into darkness when we entered a tunnel.

We'd been travelling for about an hour when the dreamboat gently tapped my foot to alert me to the vendor passing by with a trolley full of hot meals. I scrambled down the ladder. The five of us sat on the two bottom bunks as we ate from Styrofoam bowls. The elderly woman and the dreamboat's mum chatted away like old friends. I enjoyed every morsel of my fish with rice and bok choy, and then we all shared a thermos of green tea before I retreated back up to my bunk.

A bit later I ventured out of our carriage to stretch my legs while I looked for the toilets. Most people were either eating or napping. A tired-looking mother jiggled a crying baby on her lap. Two boys were playing cards on the little tables affixed beneath the windows of the aisle.

The space for the squat toilet was as cramped as a toilet on an aeroplane and the swaying motion made it difficult to balance. The stink was fetid.

After spotting a tap built into the wall near the carriage doors, I returned to my bunk to get my water bottle. I was pleased to have found a source of free water refills, but to my dismay I realised it was boiling water when my bottle started to melt in my hands. Red-faced, I turned away and saw that the person waiting behind me was holding a packet of cup noodles.

Back in the carriage, I showed the dreamboat my warped water bottle and he laughed. Then he bought me a new bottle from the next vendor that passed by.

The lights in the train went off at nine o'clock. I was lethargic from doing nothing all day and was soon lulled to sleep by the rocking motions and the clickety-clack of the wheels on the track.

When I woke the next morning, I snuggled into the starched white bedding, reminiscing about the places I'd travelled and the people I'd met. Getting out of bed was impractical to the point of being impossible, so I had all the time in the world to daydream. My confinement felt luxurious.

More bunk beds awaited me in Shanghai. I didn't relish the idea of sharing a room with nine other people, but Shanghai was one of the most expensive cities in the world and I couldn't afford my own room. A dormitory bed at Captain Hostel cost the same as a single room with a private bathroom in Phnom Penh.

I found a bottom bunk that wasn't occupied and put a t-shirt and some brochures on the pillow to claim it. The hostel had a nautical theme, with staff dressed in sailor suits and the bunks designed like the inside of a ship. Through a peephole in the bedhead, I saw a guy asleep in the bunk down from mine. He lay on his back with his mouth wide open. I gently placed my backpack in a locker and tiptoed out of the room.

I spent an hour or so exploring the riverfront promenade known as the Bund, which was lined with grand European buildings. The exquisite blend of Gothic, baroque, neoclassical and Art Deco architecture reflected Shanghai's status as a global centre of trade since the nineteenth century. Huangpu River remained as busy as ever, with cargo ships and pleasure boats plying the waters. The sky and the river were the same uninspiring shade of grey – instead it was the architecture that drew endless crowds; the promenade was filled with people smiling for photographs with the famous skyline behind them.

On the other side of the river was a huge cluster of skyscrapers that formed the business district. The most distinctive among them was the futuristic Oriental Pearl Tower. It looked like a space station, but it was actually a TV tower. Mounted on its tripod base was a large purple-and-silver dome, and above that were two silver cylinders that were connected by a series of steel ledges. Higher up was another purple dome, and at the very top, an antenna that looked like a giant syringe. I'd never seen a building like it. I wasn't sure if it was possible to go inside it – to me it seemed like a telegraph pole that could be scaled but not entered.

I strolled back to the guesthouse for sunset drinks on the rooftop bar at the hostel. According to my Lonely Planet, it was a great place to meet other travellers while enjoying superb views of the Bund.

And sure enough, I was soon talking to a couple of British guys. George was a backpacker, and James had just finished the Mongol Rally.

'What's the Mongol Rally?' I asked James, who was blond and rugged, with a short beard and hazel eyes.

'It's a car race from London to Mongolia,' he replied.

'Wow,' I said. 'That's a long way.'

'It sure is. And there's no set route, so my friend had to navigate while I drove, and vice versa. Some of the roads were in a pretty bad condition. And the rule is that you have to complete the rally in a beat-up car with a small engine, so my friend and I did it in an '89 Fiat,' he added.

'Why?'

'To make it more of an adventure.'

'How long did it take you?'

'Twenty-eight days. We travelled 10,000 miles.'

'Did you get lost?'

'Many times,' James replied with a chuckle. 'In Kazakhstan we pulled over to sleep one night, but without realising it we had crossed into Kyrgyzstan. Two teenagers with machine guns started banging on the bonnet with the butt of their rifles to wake us up. I got the fright of my life. We had to crouch down in front of their patrol car's headlights while they checked our passports.'

'Oh my god. Did they let you go?'

'After four hours. But we didn't have to pay them anything at least.'

'Far out,' I said.

'It was terrifying,' he added quite unnecessarily.

The three of us knocked back crisp Tsingtao beers as we drank in the view of the skyline. It was even more impressive at night because the muted shades of the sky and river were replaced by the contrast of darkness against the buildings' neon lights. Oriental Pearl Tower once again stole the show with its kaleidoscope of colours in flashing sequences.

'I've never stayed at a guesthouse with such an amazing view,' said James.

'Neither have I,' I replied. 'One of the places I stayed at recently didn't even have windows. Speaking of good views – would you guys fancy an even better one? My guidebook says there's a bar that's really amazing.'

'Sure,' said George and James in unison.

Twenty minutes later, we were sipping martinis on the eighty-eighth floor of Jin Mao Tower. The elevator had ascended so fast it had made my ears pop.

The view of China's biggest city from the nation's tallest building was magnificent. At three hundred and fifty metres high, we were peering down on the Oriental Pearl Tower. The bar was aptly named Cloud 9 and it was the epitome of swank, with soaring ceilings, low lighting, soft-as-butter leather chairs and, of course, floor-to-ceiling windows. At the table next to us was a woman in a black cocktail dress who was on a date with a suave-looking guy in a pencil-thin tie. They were drinking red wine from enormous crystal glasses.

I sipped my cocktail slowly, as I couldn't afford a second one. I was curious to hear what James thought of Mongolia. I told him how I'd wanted to go there ever since watching a documentary called *The Story of the Weeping Camel*. It starts with the birth of a rare white camel who is rejected by her mother. To stop it from starving, a family of nomadic shepherds travelled across the Gobi Desert to find a famed violinist. They brought him back and when he played his instrument in front of the camels, tears rolled down the mother's face and, within minutes, she had allowed her calf to suckle. The extraordinary tale was beautifully shot and nominated for an Oscar.

'It sounds like a great film,' said James. 'Mongolia is truly incredible. The grass steppes are beautiful and there's something about the sky – it just seems endless, and it's always an ethereal shade of pale blue. Even the capital city feels remote from the rest of the world. It's getting pretty cold at this time of year though.'

'Hmm. I hate the cold,' I said. 'My plan for this trip is to stay in a warm climate.'

'You can buy cashmere really cheaply in Mongolia and that will keep you warm,' suggested James.

'I guess I could,' I murmured. 'And I would love to be in a country with so many horses. I love horses. I read somewhere that Mongolia has more horses than anywhere else in the world, and hardly any people. The ratio is thirteen horses to every one human.'

'That's a fun fact.' James laughed. 'I actually met a backpacker in the capital, Ulaanbaatar, who had bought a horse from a village for about fifteen American dollars and rode it east across Mongolia. When he reached Ulaanbaatar, his guide gave him a choice: he could either sell his horse to someone else, or eat it.'

'Well, you've convinced me I should go to Mongolia,' I said. 'But I won't eat my horse.'

We took the last sips of our martinis and headed back to street level to look for a bar a fellow backpacker had told George about. It was in a converted mansion and was apparently where the cool kids of Shanghai went to party.

We walked up and down an alley three times before we

found the bar's tiny sign and nondescript entrance next to a dumpling shop. We walked up a wide set of stairs and into a mezzanine space that was brimming with beautiful people and playing house music. We took a couple of seats near the long black bar, where sparkler-clad bottles of champagne in ice buckets seemed to be the house speciality.

Everyone was so good-looking and well-dressed, yet one girl stood out among the rest. She had waist-length platinum-blonde hair and wore a backless gold lame dress that shimmered when she moved. She was so beautiful she was almost alien, with huge brown eyes and long spindly legs. I watched with fascination as she sat on a bar stool and tapped a stilettoed foot in time to the music. A guy came over and whispered something into her ear as he passed her a drink. She nodded and smiled seductively.

When we left the bar around 1 am, the place was absolutely heaving. James was leaving for Hangzhou the next day and George was off to Hong Kong, so I said goodbye and headed off to my dorm. I fumbled around in the dark for my eye mask and then slipped under the covers.

I wasn't yet asleep when a few guys came crashing in. One of them tripped over a backpack, which made the other two roar with laughter. They were completely drunk. I was expecting someone to shush them, but no one did. I warily lifted my eye mask as one of them stumbled up the ladder to the bunk bed above me. Another sat on a chair and started strumming a guitar. His friend seemed to spend forever zipping and unzipping his backpack.

Weirdos.

Finally, there was silence. I rolled over to face the wall and waited to drift off to sleep. As I kept thinking about my incredible night out, I thought I heard someone clapping. Irritated, I lifted my eye mask again. I realised it was more of a slapping.

Slap, slap, slap.

Oh my god. The guy in the bunk bed above me is masturbating.

I lay there in shock, completely grossed out. To my relief – and no doubt to his too – the wank soon ended with a muffled moan. A minute passed and he was snoring.

I was never going to stay in a dormitory again.

WHEN I OPENED my eyes the next morning, the first thing I saw was a girl with her backpack on looking confused. I sat up and smiled at her.

'Hey there. How did you get a key for the lockers?' she asked me.

'Reception gave me one when I checked in,' I replied.

'Oh right,' she said in a British accent that reminded me of a BBC newsreader. 'I wonder why we didn't get a key.'

'I'll go ask for them,' said the guy standing next to her, who I hadn't noticed until then.

He ducked off down the corridor and I swung my legs out of bed. To my relief, the bunk bed above me was empty. Its occupant had disappeared like a bad dream.

The girl introduced herself as Clementine, and said that she and her mate, Russell, had just flown in from London for a three-month trip. She was excited because it was her first taste of Asia.

Clem looked super cool. She wore a black miniskirt over three-quarter leggings and a silk scarf that matched a chunky turquoise pendant. I noticed a couple of delicate tattoos on her wrists. She was really slim, but it was her wavy tresses with honey highlights that I envied most. With my bedhead and crumpled t-shirt, a stranger would have guessed that I was the one who had just gotten off a long-haul flight.

'We're heading out to have breakfast and explore the city,' Clem said. 'Would you like to come with us?'

'I'd love to,' I said. 'Just give me five minutes to head to the bathrooms to wash my face.'

'Sure. Let's meet by the computers near the entrance.'

I was still grossed out from the night before, but I had to concede there were upsides to staying in a dormitory.

Breakfast was an incredible wonton soup at a busy eatery close to the hostel. A number of male patrons were washing down their breakfast with beers – a sight that shocked even me. After devouring the velveteen parcels of pork, I tipped my bowl up to drink every last drop of the clear broth. It had a glycerine shine and wafer-thin slices of spring onion. Every single table was full and I wasn't surprised – it was a delectable meal for less than a dollar. I resolved to go there every morning.

We returned to the Bund and bought tickets for the Shanghai Sightseeing Tunnel. We stepped into a cable car and suddenly the lights went out and a pulsating circle of gold lights shone ahead of us. A weird intergalactic voiceover started talking about the formation of planet earth and paradise and hell. Then came an evil cackle. It was all totally unexpected and Clem's confused expression had me in stitches.

We talked about our favourite art exhibitions as we wandered about a cool public art installation with curved bamboo poles stuffed into Converse sneakers, then we slowly made our way to the famous shopping strip of Nanjing Road, which is the Chinese equivalent of Fifth Avenue in New York or Oxford Street in London. The pedestrian-only thoroughfare was crawling with sightseers and high-end stores. An old man in a yellow jumpsuit grinned as he rollerskated past us – he must have been at least seventy.

We wandered into a park and tried black sesame soft serve from an ice-cream truck. Clem told me she had also recently finished a law degree. Unlike me, she planned on practising. I told her I wasn't keen to actually use my degree.

'You're not going to practise?' she said, sounding surprised.

'No.'

'What are you going to do?'

'I don't know. I love writing. But, of course, I can't make a living from it,' I added quickly.

'Maybe you could teach literature or something at a university.'

'I'd love to do that. But I'd probably need to get a PhD first.'

'Another three years of studying, huh.'

'Yeah. And I've already done six. So that would be nearly ten years all up.'

'Hmm. That's a long time. I can't say I'm madly keen on the idea of being a lawyer, but the money will be good so I'll be able to travel a lot.'

'That's a definite plus,' I said. 'I need to be able to afford to travel. I can't imagine a life without it. If I get a PhD I'll be broke for another three years.'

As we approached the Shanghai Botanic Gardens a bit later on, Clem pointed at a sign, which I read out loud.

'Respect ethic and moral codes,' I said in a stern tone. 'Do not urinate or shit.'

'Why would someone take a shit in a public park?' said Russell.

It certainly didn't seem as though the sign was necessary.

We stopped to watch a group of older couples taking tango lessons. Their teacher was playing music from a portable cassette player, so the acoustics were terrible, but the dancers were quite lovely and sweet.

Nearby was a group of men in light-blue uniforms who were sweeping up a thick layer of mud across a section of the foot-path. Russell said he'd read an article about prison work gangs being put to work in cities across China. They did menial public works jobs for free, thereby saving public funds, and their presence was a public reminder not to flout law and order. But everyone in the park was very well behaved. Not a single person was failing to abide by the multitude of signs telling visitors not to walk on the grass. To me it seemed a mean rule. Why not let people take a break from the hard concrete?

THE NEXT DAY we met up with a friend of Russell's who had studied at the same university for a couple of semesters back in the UK. Wen and her friend Lin showed us the beautiful, but crowded, Yu Gardens, which was in Old Shanghai. The collection of four-hundred-year-old buildings were exactly what came to mind when I thought of a scene from ancient China, or saw it depicted in a film. We crossed zigzag bridges to peruse decorative halls, elaborate pavilions, glittering pagodas above lime-green ponds. We did traditional tea tasting in an ancient building in Yuyuan Bazaar and browsed a souvenir emporium in the basement below. Then Wen and Lin took us to a food court to sample Shanghai specialties like sticky rice dumplings, egg crepes and soy milk custard.

Clem and I had a similar sense of humour and kept egging each other on to take dumb photos. She had first rolled her eyes at me, but agreed to stand on a pile of crushed bricks and dead tree branches after I told her with a straight face that I was shooting a 'Humans in Garbage' series. She photographed me riding a bronze lion dragon while miming that I held a pretend lasso. With Wen and Lin, we recreated the famous opening scene of *Friends* where the cast walk arm-in-arm along a footpath. I'm pretty sure Wen thought Clem and I were a bit funny in the head.

Shanghai was a fantastically fun place to explore, but it was clearly a city of contrasts. One minute I was doing my best to look cool as Clem took my photo in front of a Gucci store, and the next we were passing a row of shanties that were each the size of a closet. After taking photos of a gigantic Coca-Cola bottle embedded in the front of a five-storey building, a man passed by on a rickety bicycle – he was pulling a cart that rattled with crates of empty Coke bottles.

When we wandered into a bar to escape the humidity one afternoon, we realised it was the wrong kind of bar. About six girls appeared in little black dresses and were purring and pawing at Russell. When one tried to sit on his lap, he went bright red and couldn't get out of there fast enough.

Before dinner we checked our emails at the hostel's computers. I had an email from Gabriel, who I'd met in Hong Kong on Victoria Peak. He said a work trip to Singapore had come up unexpectedly so he was out of town. I realised I had altogether forgotten I'd emailed him. Russell wanted to send a few more emails, so Clem and I headed out for dinner together. Over noodles in a food court, I confided in her about the guy wanking in the bunk bed above me.

'Eew eew eew!' she said. 'That is revolting. You poor thing. Did you see him the next day?'

'No. He was gone by the time I got up, which was right when you and I met.'

'I guess he didn't care if anyone heard him jerking off because he knew he'd be gone in the morning. What a selfish twat,' she said.

'Totally,' I said, feeling comforted.

∼

After three fun-filled days, it was time for Clem and Russell to empty their lockers of their belongings and return the keys to reception. Before they headed downstairs for the waiting cab, we swapped email addresses, and Clem and I gave each other an especially big hug.

'Say hello to Thailand from me,' I said. 'You're going to love it.'

'I bet I will, Jess. Give me a call when you're in London. You and I will be having beers again before you know it.'

'We sure will,' I said, more brightly than I felt. Just talking about a time when my big trip was over made me sad. I reminded myself I still had so much ahead of me and squeezed Clem's hand before I let it go.

Later that afternoon, I boarded a fast train bound for Beijing. I was in high spirits, as I was excited to see the Chinese capital. My eagerness made the fourteen-hour journey seem to pass more slowly than the previous one of twenty hours. Time could be funny like that.

As the train eventually rolled into Beijing station, I stood by the doors, ready to be one of the first people off. A man with a suitcase on wheels smiled at me. He looked amused, and I knew why. I looked like a pack horse with my backpack on my back and my small day bag across my chest with water bottles tied to both sides.

The man asked me how long I'd been in China, and if I was enjoying myself. He beamed when I said I was absolutely loving it.

'Do you have a warmer jacket in your bag?' he asked me.

'Uh, no. This is all I have,' I said, gesturing to the cotton hoodie stuffed into the open compartment of my small backpack. I was arriving in Beijing during the brief time of year that was known for its clear skies and breezy days, so I hadn't thought twice about the clothes I was bringing.

'Well you better put it on before you get off the train,' he said, looking a little concerned. 'There's been a cold snap. Winter has come early this year and the nights are getting really cold. They even said on the news that it could snow in the next couple of days.'

My face fell.

I'm going to freeze.

18

FRIENDSHIPS IN THE QING DYNASTY

The man on the train was right – the air in Beijing was icy cold. I blew into my hands to warm them up as I started off on foot towards the guesthouse. The sky was clear and a brilliant blue, and soon enough I was perspiring from the effort of carrying my heavy pack. I'd go buy some warmer clothes once I was free of it.

As I got closer to the guesthouse, I entered a maze of tiny laneways that were surrounded by grey stone walls. I was in a historic neighbourhood known as a hutong, which are alleys formed by rows of traditional courtyard homes joined up to one another. They had first sprung up in the thirteenth century, which was also when Beijing became the dynastic capital of China.

The hutong was bustling with life and dappled sunshine streamed through the leaves of gnarled old wisteria trees. A rickshaw almost brushed my shoulder as it overtook me along the bumpy cobblestone path.

Every few metres along the impenetrable walls were sets of maroon double doors, many adorned with calligraphy and beautiful brass handles. Most were closed, but an open set revealed a leafy courtyard where a woman was hanging out the washing. Two little boys pushed toy cars along the smooth stone surface and an old man sat watching them as he smoked a cigarette with a terrier asleep at his feet.

After several twists and turns, I reached Lusongyuan Hotel. It looked more like a temple than a place to stay, with imposing red columns, a patterned sloping roof and a landscape painting on a porcelain frieze above its grand red doors. At the base of the steps were two grey, stone lions resting on their haunches. A dozen red lanterns dangled from the eaves.

I stepped into a shadowy corridor and a woman on reception greeted me warmly in English. She told me there was a free bed in one of the dormitories down the back of the hotel. I missed having my own private space, but the social aspect of staying in a dormitory was a big upside and it saved me money. Plus Lusongyuan Hotel was listed in my Lonely Planet as one of the most popular places for budget travellers to stay in Beijing. It was originally built by a Mongolian general during the Qing dynasty, which began way back in the seventeenth century. I had a few good reasons to give communal living another go.

I was certain I'd made the right choice when I walked into a stunning traditional courtyard. It looked like something Marco Polo would have described from his travels along the Silk Road when he stayed at caravanserais, with its shuttered red doors, intricate latticework and potted bonsais. A dozen or so travellers were chatting away at the tables and chairs set up around the peaceful oasis.

There was only a top bunk left in the dormitory, so I put some of my stuff on it and headed back out to buy a jumper and check out Tiananmen Square. It was within Dongcheng District, which is where the hotel was, so I didn't have far to go. Nevertheless I set out with trepidation. The idea of navigating the world's most populous capital city was intimidating. Beijing covered an area that was significantly larger than Shanghai and with a population of 21 million, it had almost as many people as the whole of Australia. I told myself I should be able to get myself to the closest metro station if I became hopelessly lost.

To my relief, finding Tiananmen Square was fairly straightforward, as the choked roads outside the hutong ran along a grid. Soon enough, the world's biggest public square was in view. It was a vast expanse of pavement, with hordes of tourists posing in front of an enormous portrait of Chairman Mao hanging on Tiananmen Gate. This was where Mao proclaimed the founding of the People's Republic of China in 1949, and his body lay in state nearby at the mausoleum. Having already seen one embalmed state leader, I didn't feel the need to see another.

Facing the square was the massive National Museum of China. Under its Stalinist columns was a gigantic stopwatch that was as big as a bus. It displayed information in both English and Mandarin and it was counting down the hours, minutes and seconds until the 2008 Beijing Olympics. The sporting event was another two years off, so a countdown seemed more like an exercise in patience than generating buzz. However, I knew the Chinese have a predilection for taking a long view of history – and there was so much of it for them to glean from. While studying international relations at university, I'd heard a story about the first Chinese premier, Zhou Enlai being asked by a journalist about the impact of the French Revolution.

'It's too soon to say,' he'd apparently quipped.

In Australia, it sometimes felt as if our politicians didn't think beyond their four-year terms, which could make domestic politics seem myopic. It's not that I wanted to live in a one-party state like China, but I admired it for being the world's oldest continuous civilisation with 4000 years of recorded history. To keep such a large swathe of territory unified as one country for so long was extraordinary.

Of course, Tiananmen Square was an example of the brutal measures deployed to quash dissent. It had been almost twenty years since pro-democracy protestors had been gunned down in the square, but the place was crawling with police. Sinister-looking CCTV cameras were attached to every lamp post, and, apparently, plainclothes police patrolled the area day and night, blending in with the tourist groups, power walkers and kids flying kites. The Chinese state was vigilant in preventing any kind of repeat occurrence of 1989.

I was standing right where one of the most iconic photographs of the twentieth century had been taken. The image of a lone man facing a row of military tanks was on the cover of a book I'd read about the Tiananmen Square massacre and I used to stare at it all the time. The image sums up the extraordinary power imbalance between the individual and the state, as well as the unidentified man's courage to risk everything for a better future. He became known as 'Tank Man' and I shudder to think what may have happened to him.

Inside China, the uprising and subsequent crackdown of 1989 had been erased from history. The heavily censored internet returned zero results for the search term 'Tiananmen Square massacre' and public awareness was low to non-existent. I thought China would be stronger if it embraced democracy, but I wouldn't dare voice such an opinion out loud while I was there.

It was dusk when I got back to the guesthouse. I went over to a small group of travellers in the courtyard and asked if I could have a seat.

'Of course,' said a girl with a sandy-brown bob, patting the chair next to her. 'Would you like a glass of Great Wall?'

'Great Wall?' I asked.

'Red wine. Cheap red wine.' She grinned.

'Sure, thanks a lot.'

She filled up a plastic cup and passed it to me. 'I'm Bethan,' she said, looking at me with intelligent green eyes. 'I'm from Wales. I've just come off the Trans-Siberian Railway.'

'How amazing!' I exclaimed. 'Did you take it all the way from Moscow?'

'Yup.'

'I loved Paul Theroux's book that describes his experiences on it – *The Great Railway Bazaar*.'

'I've read that too – it's great. I've wanted to make the journey for years and I'm so glad I got to do it. I'll start a new job at a different university next year, so the timing was perfect.'

'Were there many other backpackers onboard?' I asked.

'Only a few. Actually, I didn't really have much company. The women in my compartment laughed at me when I spoke Russian. They told me not to bother. I didn't have much luck with anyone on the train, actually.'

'They laughed at you when you tried to speak their language?' I asked incredulously.

'Yeah, they did. And the thing is I learned Russian up to university level, so it's not as though I'm a hopeless beginner.'

'I'm shocked. Anytime I've tried to speak a language like Khmer or Vietnamese, the response has been so positive and encouraging. I feel self-conscious when I try to speak a foreign language – being laughed at would completely put me off.'

'Yeah, it did put me off,' she said. 'I kind of take the Russians with a grain of salt though. They're a grumpy bunch. If you people-watch on the streets of Moscow, everyone appears to be scowling. There's even a Russian proverb: "A smile without a reason is a sign of idiocy." Anyhow, the scenery was incredible. It was so pristine and stark. There were times when I couldn't make out what was land and what was sky, as everything was covered in snow.'

I told Bethan I hadn't realised it would be so cold in Beijing, and that I'd bought the jumper and beanie I was wearing just that afternoon because I had no warm clothes.

'Wait here,' said Bethan and she ran off to her dorm.

She came back and handed me a thermal top and pants, plus a soft woollen jumper.

'We're the same size. Plus I'm headed for the tropics next so you'll be lightening my load if you take them,' she said.

I accepted the clothes gratefully and we poured ourselves another wine.

A guy called Josiah from Oregon came and sat next to Bethan. He had long hair under a fedora hat and wore a baggy, navy-blue shirt. I was soon laughing my head off as he described how he'd bumbled around New Zealand in a campervan. Thailand and Laos were next on his list, although he was running low on funds and wasn't sure if he'd be away the full year he'd planned.

Josiah introduced us to Phil and Bruce – a pair of handsome bearded friends who had just finished the Mongol Rally. With them was a blonde from Germany called Yvonne, who I later learned had hooked up with Phil the night before.

We had just pushed the two tables together when a guy with a shaved head arrived.

'Any takers?' he asked in a broad Aussie accent, holding up what looked like a big bottle of vinegar.

'Oh god – tonight? I can't face it. Oh all right – maybe I will,' said Bruce with a chuckle.

'What is it?' I asked.

'It's baijiu. It's China's national drink. People drink it at banquets and stuff. This one is made from fermented rice,' he replied.

'Ah – it sounds like the Lao-Lao I had in Laos,' I said.

'Pretty much,' replied the Australian. 'It's nice to hear an Aussie accent. You can have the first pour. I'm Luke, by the way.' He held out a plastic cup.

'Thanks, Luke,' I said. 'I'm Jess – and I'm probably going to regret this.'

After three shots of the firewater over the course of the next hour or so, I challenged Josiah to a kung-fu match. I tried to intimidate him by boasting that I'd had a lesson. He joked that he was willing to take the risk, as he had watched a lot of Jackie Chan movies.

Under the soft glow of red lamps, we circled each other like hungry hyenas. Bruce gave mock sporting commentary on our softly-softly jabs and pathetic leaps. I tried a surprise sideways kick and lost my balance – though at least I brought Josiah down with me. We were holding our sides laughing on the cobblestones.

'Get up you two – it's time for a science experiment,' said Luke. 'I want to find out if this baijiu has a high enough alcohol content to catch on fire.'

'At sixty per cent alcohol, I hypothesise that it will,' said Phil. 'And at eleven yuan a litre, we can afford to find out.'

A few other backpackers came over to watch. Phil stood beside Luke with a notebook and a silly grin on his face. Luke squatted level with the table, then tipped the clear liquid into a small glass.

'Assistant – lighter, please,' he said to Phil.

Luke struck a match and held it close to the glass. A small flame began to lick the corners of the glass, much like a sambuca shot.

'It burns!' we yelled excitedly.

~

I MET UP WITH JOSIAH, Bethan, Luke, Bruce, Phil and Yvonne the next morning. We had breakfast and hired rusty bicycles from the stack leaning against the sides of the wall. We wandered through the Forbidden City, which had served as the home of Chinese emperors for five hundred years, right up until the end of the Qing dynasty in 1912. The temple complex was teeming with tourists and I found it less interesting than the hutongs, where communities still lived.

Nearby were row upon row of souvenir shops selling Chairman Mao merchandise on an industrial scale. We perused the watches, clocks, caps, plates, mugs, magnets, cigarette lighters and key rings. You name it – Mao's face was on it. It made the Ho Chi Minh souvenir range in Vietnam look like a cottage industry. I bought a parchment with beautiful calligraphy to post to Mum and Dad.

Bethan told me about a new book she'd read about Mao by Jung Chang, the author of the award-winning *Wild Swans*. Bethan said that Mao secretly wanted to dominate the world, and he poisoned anyone who stood in his way. By bringing about the biggest famine in history, he caused the deaths of 38 million people. I listened, flabbergasted, noticing she'd lowered her voice as she told me about the book, even though the chances of anyone either overhearing or comprehending her words were small.

After a stroll around Jingshan Park, we passed the late afternoon lounging on comfy couches at the bar in the guesthouse, which was showing a Hollywood film starring Brad Pitt and Angelina Jolie. It had been months since I'd chilled out with a movie. I braided Josiah's hair and Bethan added a couple of pink feathers.

Being a good sport, Josiah kept his new hairstyle as we headed off to the Beijing Pop Festival that night. We were close to the stage for Supergrass, although the view was impeded by what Luke referred to as the 'Chinese fun police'. They stood stone-faced and shoulder-to-shoulder in a long row facing the concertgoers. Some of them were baby-faced, but they were outwardly unmoved by the music. The crowd was anything but. When Supergrass played their hit song 'Alright' from the movie *Clueless*, we all went crazy.

'Soundtrack to our life!' shouted Luke.

It felt so good to get a long-overdue dose of rock music. As we walked home, I told Phil that I wanted to stay in Asia somehow.

'And I want to avoid another boring office job for as long as I possibly can,' I said.

'You should teach English in Korea,' he said. 'Bruce and I are thinking of doing it. I met some travellers the other day who teach in Seoul. They said the pay is really good and you work part-time, plus you get free board. Native English speakers are always in demand. You just need the qualification to teach English as a foreign language. I can give you the contacts they gave me if you want.'

'That would be amazing,' I said excitedly, and began walking with an extra spring in my step.

I GOT UP EARLY the next morning and took the metro to the passport office, where I submitted an application to extend my visa for a second month. After a rough start, I now wanted to see as much of the vast country as I could, and in Beijing I had found my tribe. Afterwards I went to an internet café and sent a gushing group email about my new friends to my old friends. I attached photos of us doing dumb stuff like hugging trees in the park and trying on wigs at a jumble store. Then I replied to an email I'd received a few days earlier from Carol, who was a friendly manager I'd reported to at the publishing company.

'I have no idea how you are going to be able to stop travelling and do the "normal" thing, Jess! Your travel adventures sound so excellent,' she wrote.

Carol was right.

'I don't know how I'll be able to settle down again – even in England,' I wrote back. 'I'm actually now thinking of teaching English for a year in South Korea, Taiwan or Japan. I could make good money, be overseas, work part-time and use the rest of the week to do some of my own writing. Maybe after that I could move to England with enough money to study something like literature or history – or maybe journalism or editing?! But I'm a bit confused, as you can probably see. Maybe I will just settle into London at a publishing company and be happy. But I do hope that I can delay the office just a bit longer...'

It seemed like a terrific plan to me, although I knew Mum and Dad wouldn't share my enthusiasm. They had booked flights to London where we planned to meet up at the end of my travels. I had to at least be there when they arrived. Didn't I? They would be so upset if I cancelled. But even if I did stick to the plan, my parents wouldn't exactly be thrilled if I told them I wasn't settling down after an entire year of travelling; a period of time they considered decadent.

When I got back to the hotel my friends were sitting around a table in the courtyard. They were laughing about something, although that in itself wasn't unusual.

'Stop it, Bruce,' said Phil, affectionately shoving his shoulder. 'Give me your camera so I can delete the photos.'

'No way,' said Bruce, holding the camera out of his reach. 'I'll stop taking photos of your bare white arse if you promise me I won't have to listen to you having sex with Yvonne tonight in the dorm.'

'I'm not going to make any promises. Keep the damn photos,' Phil replied, and laughed.

I glanced at Yvonne, whose freckled complexion didn't show even the hint of a blush. She took a sip of coffee and put out her cigarette.

'Anyhow,' she said, clearing her throat. 'I met a French girl this morning called Sabine who is going to camp overnight at the Great Wall tomorrow. We will watch the sunrise. Who wants to come?'

'Are tourists allowed to stay overnight?' I asked.

'No, they're not. But Sabine said they only have guards patrolling at the main tourist areas. She knows someone else who did it.'

'It would be an amazing experience,' I said. 'I'll come with you.'

'I'm too lazy to join you, but let's meet up the next morning,' said Phil.

Yvonne and I began plotting our secret expedition, but in the end I chickened out. The prospect of spending a night in freezing temperatures didn't appeal, nor did getting caught by Chinese police. I considered myself pretty adventurous, but Yvonne was in another league.

After a two-hour drive that began at dawn, we met Yvonne at the starting point to a section of the wall known as Mutianyu, which was well preserved and less touristy than the other nearby option of Bataling.

Yvonne and I jumped in a cable car, with Bruce, Phil and Josiah in the car behind us. As the contraption rattled and groaned and our feet dangled above the dry scrub of the ravine below, Yvonne told me that she and Sabine had ended up sleeping in a watchtower because they couldn't get their tent up. The night otherwise passed without incident, and she said the sunrise had been magnificent.

'Oh look!' I squealed, as I caught sight of the wall.

I was so excited to see another world wonder, and it looked just as it did in pictures, with the incomprehensibly long wall reminding me of dominoes stretched across the undulating hills and punctuated with watchtowers. The next world wonder I'd get to see would likely be the Taj Mahal, I thought with relish.

As I took in the panoramic view, I told Yvonne how I really wanted to go to Mongolia after China, but I was worried that I'd be too cold, as winter was approaching.

'I wouldn't rate Mongolia all that highly,' she said. 'Ulaanbaatar is ugly and it's so polluted. It's also absolutely freezing. Winter this year has come freakishly early, so it was before the usual date the government switches on the electricity generator to cope with the extra demand. There was basically no heating and I froze my butt off. To be honest, I didn't really like it.'

'Ah, fair enough,' I said. 'I've met some people who have absolutely raved about it, which made me want to go there. I've also heard that it is a paradise for horse lovers like me.'

'I think my time there was spoiled because I got bitten by a street dog during my second week. I got eight stitches on my arse. I hadn't been vaccinated for rabies before I left home, so I had just twenty-four hours to fly out to Beijing and get a rabies shot.'

I looked at her, horrified. I couldn't believe she hadn't mentioned any of this until now.

'How's the wound now?' I asked.

'It's much less painful than it was; I can tell you that. But I keep telling Phil not to grab my arse and he forgets,' she added with a laugh.

She is in a completely different league, I thought to myself once again.

We spent the next five hours hiking ten kilometres along the 2000-year-old wall, and it was a most unusual workout. The wall was six metres wide and had been built by independent kingdoms to keep out marauding nomads from the capital. The steps were of wildly different sizes, with steep up and down slopes. Some of the steps were broken and crumbling. As I clambered along it while trying hard not to roll an ankle, I was once again filled with awe about how things in China are built to last.

We took frequent breaks to catch our breath – and, of course, to take tonnes of photos. During one such break, an old man – his face lined like the creases in an elephant's skin – approached us offering cans of Snow Beer and cigarettes. He was as nimble as a mountain goat but it must be such a tough way for an elderly man to make a living. He wore a bottle-green cap with a red star like Mao and he obliged me by sitting next to me for a photo. He gave a toothless smile for the camera. Bruce passed him a couple of yuan for a packet of Double Happiness cigarettes.

'Tastes like sawdust,' he said, chuckling as he inhaled.

The incongruously-named cigarettes came in a gold package with embossed red lettering. Some of the cigarette packets I'd seen were works of art, with richly coloured designs with a metallic sheen. There was an extraordinary range on offer too, with dozens of brands on the market.

During the bus ride back to Beijing, I fell asleep with my head on Josiah's shoulder. He gently woke me up when we got back to the hotel. I was so exhausted I tumbled into my bunk bed fully dressed.

A WEEK PASSED before any of us contemplated moving on from Beijing. We didn't do everything together, but we always ended the day as a group, drinking and mucking about in the courtyard.

The weather was especially beautiful one afternoon, so I headed out to the hutong alone with my camera. I stopped at a street-food stall and filled up on roubing, which is flatbread filled with finely chopped pork. I walked and walked and walked, and it was a wonderful afternoon. I realised that while I still had no idea what was going on around me and had to use sign language for basic transactions, I could definitely see the funny side of it all. It was like some long-running game of charades. Perhaps the difference was that in this city I knew I was meeting up with my friends that night and could have a laugh about any misunderstandings I'd had.

I met my friends at a restaurant that was famous for its delicious Peking duck. The dish was a speciality of Beijing, which was known as Peking until 1986. I happily announced that my visa extension had been approved, and that I had decided against going to Mongolia. Yvonne's description had put me off, and travelling to Mongolia would take me off course for reaching India, which was the only country I definitely had in my sights when I first set off from Australia.

My new plan was to travel to an autonomous region called Inner Mongolia. It would give me a taste of Mongolian culture while keeping within China and on track for making it to India.

'That will be great, Jess,' said Bethan. 'You can tell us whether it's a weird imitation or the real thing.'

'Let's make a toast. To China and the best people I've met on my travels so far,' said Josiah.

'To friendships in the Qing dynasty,' joked Luke.

We clinked our beer bottles and a whole duck arrived on our table. I wrapped slice after slice of the rich dark meat inside a pancake, drizzling it with a generous serve of plum sauce and batons of cucumber.

With full bellies, we returned to the courtyard at

Lusongyuan Hotel. I opened a beer, but couldn't finish it. I was pretty wiped out and headed to bed instead of kicking on.

Twenty minutes later I was sprinting across the courtyard to the toilets, whose location I rued. I returned to my bunk, but minutes later I was hotfooting it down the ladder again.

'Are you okay?' asked Bethan, looking concerned.

'Yeah, I'm okay,' I replied in a small voice as I slunk back to my bunk.

But no sooner was I back in bed than the dreaded gurgling in my bowels started up again. Fearing a repeat of the night I had duck fetus in Cambodia, I swung on my backpack and went to the front desk to ask for a single room. None were available, so I hauled myself across the laneway to another hotel. To my immense relief, within minutes I was putting my pack down in a single room. It was expensive, but I had little choice. I made it just in time. But my relief soon turned to despair when I began vomiting.

Was the duck fetus in Cambodia reincarnated into a Peking duck to strike me down a second time?

But it was no joke. I felt like a crab was twisting its pincers inside my stomach. The pain was terrible and I couldn't stop vomiting.

When the sun finally rose after a night that had felt never-ending, I was feeling worse than ever. On top of the vomiting and diarrhoea was a sore throat, lower back pain, and a strange ringing sensation in my ears. I cried while continuing to throw up bile. I needed medical attention.

19

DOUBLE HAPPINESS

I walked through the automatic doors of Beijing Friendship Hospital and approached the nurses behind the counter with a weak smile. They wore pastel-pink uniforms with pillbox hats. One of the nurses said something to her colleagues as she came towards me, then motioned for me to follow her. I felt calmer just for being inside a health facility, but I was weak and found it difficult to keep up with her. I shuffled across seemingly endless corridors and a skywalk as though I was headed for a geriatric ward.

At last we came to a consulting room, where the nurse indicated I should wait. I sat alone for about ten minutes before a doctor came in and looked at me with obvious curiosity.

'What is wrong with you?' he asked kindly.

I was so delighted to have found an English-speaking doctor that the words tumbled out.

'I've had vomiting and diarrhoea all night long after eating Peking duck at a restaurant with some friends. In all likelihood, I probably got sick from the street-food snack I had before dinner, because none of my friends were sick and we ate the same duck.

I also have a sore throat, lower back pain, and my ears are ringing.'

'Mmm-hmm.'

He reached into a drawer and pulled out a lightweight hammer. He came round to my side of the desk and went tap, tap, tap. He nodded and sat down again, and then started writing in a thin notebook. He asked me to write my name in a box on the front page, which had a photo of the hospital on it. The only other thing I understood was the single word 'OK' followed by an exclamation mark. Everything else was, of course, in Chinese.

'What colour is your urine today?' the doctor asked me.

'Uh, it's yellow,' I stammered.

'Light yellow or dark yellow?'

'I'm not sure.'

'When we wake up in the morning and go to the toilet, it's normal for our urine to be dark yellow. Over the course of the day it gets lighter.'

He handed me a sample jar and I went and peed in the toilets down the corridor.

When he held up the warm contents of the jar up to the light, he shook his head and said, 'It is the wrong colour. If the colour doesn't change by Friday, you'll need to return for liver-functioning testing.'

'Okay,' I said, feeling worried.

He continued making notes and wrote me a prescription for various medicines, including tablets for pain and fever, tablets for what he called 'weakness', along with ear drops and cough syrup. I didn't understand why I was getting cough syrup because I hadn't mentioned having a cough, but I was nonetheless glad that he was covering all bases.

The doctor dipped a brush into a pot of glue and stuck bits

of tissue paper in the back of the notebook – I figured these were the bills for the medicines. He handed me the scrapbook (which I ended up taking home as a souvenir). I was surprised and pleased that the bill only amounted to around fifteen dollars.

I slept deeply back in my hotel for a few hours and then headed out to send an email to Mum and Dad. There was a convenience store along the alleyway that had a few computers on the back wall. It was only a five-minute walk from the hotel, but the bright light of the sun hurt my eyes and the smells wafting up from the drains almost made me vomit.

The girl at the internet café greeted me like an old friend, as she seemed to for everyone who walked through the door. She spoke a little English, although it was mostly the words of the items she sold in the store. I bought some plain crackers and told her I was sick by looking pained as I clutched my stomach.

Hey Mum and Dad

I am feeling a bit miserable because I was sick all night. I have no energy and lots of cramps. I went to a hospital and the doctor said I may need liver-functioning testing. He gave me loads of tablets. I stayed in an expensive hotel last night because I didn't want to be sick in the dorm.

I've decided not to go to Mongolia as it will be freezing cold. It would also take me in the wrong direction from India.

I guess I'm lucky that I haven't been sick for quite a while now. But I would love a hug! A hotel room doesn't have the same comforting atmosphere you crave when you're sick...

Miss you lots

Jess xx

. . .

By the next morning the tablets had kicked in, so I went to Lusongyuan Hotel to let the others know I was doing better. Then I checked my emails again. There was a reply from Mum, who was, of course, worried about me.

Hi Jess

I'm sorry to hear that you're feeling so sick. Are you going back to the doctor? Someone said Coca-Cola is good for stomach upsets, as are ginger drinks. The back pain may be related to kidneys and dehydration so you have to tell the doctor about that pain. Your liver is taking a beating. You have to stop drinking alcohol – even when you feel well again.

Do you claim on travel insurance for your medical bills? Don't cut corners to save money. Your health is the most important thing you have and I feel you are playing Russian roulette with it. Just tell us if you need help with money.

That's good about not going to Mongolia. But India is going to be even harder than China – your mother is not happy. I think about you heaps and I know you have this restless, wild spirit like your Uncle Alec – but I wish you wouldn't do half the stuff you do. You will understand one day when you are a mother!

Why don't you get off to England while the weather is still good? You could settle in before the winter.

I will check emails again tonight and I hope for better news of you.

Hope to hear from you, baby girl.
Love Mummy xxx

It was so nice to get sympathy from Mum, but I also realised we had vastly different ideas about what I should do next. There was no way I'd even consider cutting my trip short to go to England – I was thinking of skipping it altogether. Mum had always said that I was like Philip's dad Alec – he had left school at sixteen to go to sea and he ended up a ship captain. Perhaps she was right. I never wanted to stay in one place all my life.

In truth, my enthusiasm for teaching in South Korea had waned, but that was probably only because I was sick. I felt confused and guilty and just sent Mum a vague reply saying the cramps had started to subside.

I asked the girl at the café if she knew of a cheap hotel, as I couldn't face returning to the dorm. I'd had a taste of the privacy of a single room, and it was still touch and go with my toilet requirements. She gave me the business card for a budget hotel.

I was shown a room with two single beds that faced a small courtyard. It was more than I had hoped to spend on accommodation, but I took it anyway.

After three days of eating mostly steamed rice and crackers, I felt like my old self again. Paying no heed to Mum's advice to stop drinking, I swung back into Beijing's night scene with renewed enthusiasm. One night we went clubbing at a massive place called the Banana Club. Bruce and I capped off the bender by buying one last bottle of Great Wall at dawn from the convenience store. We were still drinking in the courtyard at my hotel when travellers began to emerge bleary-eyed for a day at the Great Wall. Bruce and I made out in my hotel room, but it was a one-off and not the start of anything romantic.

I was still a regular at the courtyard and bar at Lusongyuan Hotel, even though I wasn't a paying guest. We drank baijiu and beers every evening and I played around on the DJ decks next to the bar. I also made some new friends.

Lucio was a blues player from New Orleans who played the guitar or saxophone at the guesthouse bar each evening. He was about ten years older than me and had been in Beijing for three months. He took me out for lunch at a restaurant in Sanlitun in Chaoyang district, which is one of Beijing's wealthiest neighbourhoods. Most of the embassies and international organisations are located there, and its restaurants and bars are geared towards expats. We dined al fresco and as it was a sunny Saturday afternoon, there were loads of people out and about. I sipped a glass of white wine and twirled spaghetti on my fork as Lucio told me about how he travelled the world, giving live performances at guesthouses in return for free board. His goal was to learn about as many different styles of world music as possible. I wished I had a skill like that to barter.

Lucio had experienced racism in China, with some taxi drivers refusing to take him as a passenger. One guy in a shop had made derogatory comments about him being an African, and customs officials had probed him with unnecessary questions.

I said how sorry I was to hear that, and Lucio shrugged and changed the subject. He began talking about what a travesty it was that many hutongs were being flattened ahead of the Olympics. The Chinese government considered them at odds with the image of modernity they wanted to project to the world. I agreed that it was madness to destroy them.

That night, a big group of us from the guesthouse watched Lucio perform at a swanky bar called CD Jazz Café. It was tucked behind the Agricultural Exhibition Centre and I would never have known it existed without an invitation from Lucio. I could see how sticking around in a city led to a much deeper familiarity with it than what I ever saw as a backpacker.

After yet another fantastic night out in Beijing, I said goodnight to my friends at Lusongyuan Hotel and began walking back to my hotel room along the alleyway. It was peaceful and very few people were out. I was still humming a jazz ditty and I didn't pay much notice to the two men ahead of me, who were bent over and engrossed in their task.

When I drew up close to them, I stopped in my tracks. A dead dog lay on a metal tray. It had been a big dog, and its skin had been glazed like a Peking duck. Its legs were bent as though it had been killed while running, and its mouth was open. One of the men was tapping out its teeth with a hammer.

I was so shocked that I wasn't looking where I was going and almost tripped over a second dog that was lying on the pavement. A pool of blood trickled from its body into the drain.

As I got into bed a little later, I willed myself to forget what I had seen. But I knew that the image of the cooked dogs would stay with me forever.

WE BEGAN our final night together in Beijing as we always did: with some drinks in the courtyard. I started talking to a German guy called Bert. I liked him immediately as he had a gentle sort of kindness about him. In a few hours he would be hopping aboard the new long-distance train to Tibet. His plan was to spend three months learning Tibetan at a local university in the capital city of Lhasa. His girlfriend Franziska was travelling through Asia and was due to meet him there in a week.

However, Bert didn't have much money and so he had purchased a ticket for a seat rather than a sleeper, and he was travelling on a slow, old train rather than a bullet train. Lhasa is 4500 kilometres from Beijing, so Bert would be sitting up for the equivalent of three days straight! I wouldn't even have contemplated such a long and uncomfortable journey, but he didn't seem at all phased.

When I repeated how cool I thought it was to be going to Tibet, Bert replied: 'Why don't you go there?'

'Well, I don't know. It's so far away,' I replied.

'You don't have to go there directly as I am – you could stop at some of the amazing places in central China along the way. There's Xi'an and Pingyao and Chengdu...'

'Well, yes – that does sound like a fantastic idea,' I said, thinking it over. 'Plus Tibet shares a border with Nepal, and Nepal shares a border with India, so I'd be heading in the right direction.'

'So why don't you come? Franziska will be there for the next few months. We can meet up.'

I paused for a couple of seconds.

'Okay – I will! I'm going to go to Tibet!' I exclaimed.

I hugged my new friend goodbye with a promise to see him soon, and then headed out to a South Korean restaurant with Bruce, Phil, Luke, Josiah and Bethan. Phil and Yvonne had ended their fling, and Yvonne had apparently left Beijing pretty quickly after that.

We ordered some beers and scanned the menu; bypassing the various dishes that featured dog meat. I shuddered again. I'd seen pedigree pets in China that appeared to be the apple of their owner's eyes, but the widespread cruelty to other kinds of animals had shocked and saddened me. It had started on my first day with the bear paws at the restaurant in the border town, and then the zoo in Guilin with the sad monkey and tiny enclosures for all creatures. There was also a squirrel in a teeny tiny cage in the hotel courtyard. I hated to observe its miserable existence and was constantly fighting an urge to open the hatch and let it out.

After munching on fried chicken and talking about the fun we'd have together as English teachers in South Korea once our travels were over, we started walking back towards the hutong. As we waited for a green light for pedestrians at a huge intersection, I caught sight of a man on the other side of the road. He was poking a stick into a fish tank, which was sitting atop a trolley cart. As we crossed the road and came closer to him, I saw there were two tiny ginger kittens inside the tank. They were covered in their own excrement and were clawing at the glass with terrified eyes. I couldn't stand to see yet another animal suffering and do nothing about it.

'I'm going to buy the kittens,' I said impulsively, and walked over to the man before my friends had time to stop me.

After a bit of back-and-forth to work out how much he was charging for the two kittens, I gave him the equivalent of fifteen dollars. He scooped up each kitten and put them in a couple of shoeboxes. I was now a pet owner in Beijing.

When we got back to Lusongyuan Hotel, I released the kittens into the courtyard and watched with satisfaction as they realised they were free and cautiously began to explore their new surroundings. In a matter of minutes, the kittens were feasting on salami and canned tuna that backpackers had retrieved from their personal stores. Someone else gave them a ping pong ball to chase around.

Phil came down the road with me to drop the kittens off at my hotel before we headed out to a bar. I wrapped my jacket around the shoeboxes and Phil and I raised our voices and pretended to laugh to prevent the owner hearing any miaowing as we walked past the front desk.

The kittens leaped onto my bed and began licking themselves clean. I sighed happily as they started frolicking together on the floor. I was overjoyed to watch the sudden change in fortune for them.

'I'm going to stay in tonight, Phil,' I said. 'I just want to play with them and cuddle them.'

'No way, Jess!' He replied. 'It's our last night together as a group. Don't be mad. They will be here when you get home.'

'That's true,' I said, still a little reluctantly. 'I'll just draw the curtains so the owners don't see them.'

Going out ended up a wise move, because I got talking to a guy while waiting in line for a drink. I told him I had just adopted two cats and he laughed and said he had four at home. Taking two more would be no problem. He said his name was Qian and wrote down his phone number. I grinned and said I'd call in the morning to arrange a time to drop off the kittens. I couldn't believe my luck. Problem solved! I was then able to focus on having one last night of fun with the people I'd grown so close to over the past eleven days. It was an emotional farewell at the end of the night, with a big group hug and pledges made to see each other again as soon as possible.

MY HEAD WAS THROBBING when I opened my eyes the next morning, but I smiled when I saw the kittens curled up on the chair like two little peaceful fluff balls. I sniffed the air – what was that? The kittens had shat on my blanket! Both of them! Gross.

I swallowed a couple of Panadol – it had been a very late night – and then I went and showered. I threw the ping pong ball around the room and the kittens hurtled after it. Watching them play would never get old, but I had to swing into action.

I gave Qian a call from the nearby phone booth. It rang out, so I tried again. No answer. I drummed my fingers on the glass as I started to panic. My train was leaving for Inner Mongolia in just six hours' time. I was itching to move on after staying in one place for longer than usual and trains to Hohhot were infrequent. But I couldn't abandon the kittens less than twelve hours after I'd rescued them. That would be horribly irresponsible. I had to find someone who would look at them and see double happiness.

I tried the manager at Lusongyuan Hotel, but she quickly declined. So I headed out to ask the friendly girl at the shop with the computers if she would like a couple of free kittens. I did this by meowing and holding up two fingers, and then I pointed at her and gestured towards my hotel. In China, holding up the pinkie finger means you want to go to the toilet, so I wasn't certain how she would interpret me holding up two fingers – I hoped I wasn't inadvertently telling her something I didn't mean to. Somehow she seemed to understand me. The young woman beamed and nodded, then made a phone call. In less than a minute another young girl, who I assumed was a friend or sister, had showed up to mind the shop.

We walked along the alleyway to my hotel, stopping on the way to ask her mother (so I assumed) who worked at the laundromat (I think) for permission. She seemed even more excited when she came out, and on we went.

When I brought the kittens into the courtyard, I didn't make any attempt to conceal them. They were going to their new home so it was all good. But to my dismay, I saw the girl's expression had turned to mild horror. I guess she hadn't understood there were two little darlings.

'Double happiness?' I said, already knowing it was a lost cause.

She took a few steps backwards and almost bumped into the hotel owner as he came around the corner. To my delight, he smiled. As the shop girl left the premises with an apologetic wave, he opened his arms and I handed him the kittens. I asked him if he would like to keep them and he nodded.

With an enormous sense of relief, I checked out of my room and left my backpack behind the front desk while I headed out for one last meal in Beijing and to make a call home to Mum and Dad.

By the time I came back to grab my backpack and head to the train station, the kittens were lapping up milk from porcelain saucers while the hotel owner gently stroked them. We smiled at one another as I fastened the strap of my pack across my waist. Having been freed from the shackles of pet ownership, I was ready to board the train for Inner Mongolia.

20

IN OR OUT?

As I walked the streets of downtown Hohhot in search of a travel agency, I felt further than five hundred kilometres from Beijing. I was still in East Asia, but the capital city of Inner Mongolia had Central Asian influences too, such as the cumin seed flatbread I bought from a hawker with ruddy cheeks and a fur hat. I passed a Muslim restaurant with Arabic lettering on the front of its yellow-and-green facade, and many street signs and shops featured Mongolian script as well as Mandarin. With its loops, twirls and thick flourishes, Mongolian looked more similar to Arabic than Chinese. In actual fact, the top-down script is an adaptation of classical Uyghur, which is spoken in an area not far to the west.

The winds that blew in from the Russian border to the northeast were icy cold, so I was glad to soon be inside a travel agency. It was crammed with boxes of brochures and a thick film of dust covered the window panes. Hohhot is the main jumping-off point for tours of the grasslands, so I was able to get a ticket for a two-day tour that began the following morning.

I wasn't enthusiastic about going on a tour because I preferred to move at my own pace, however there was no other way to access the grasslands. The upside was that I was guaranteed to sleep inside a ger, which is a circular tent insulated with felts. The Russian term of 'yurt' is better known. I had read that Inner Mongolia was a bit of a tourist trap for mainland Chinese tourists, but I was nonetheless excited to get a glimpse of the Land of the Weeping Camel.

I walked into a noodle shop and a customer almost dropped her chopsticks when she saw me. The girls at the cash register were giggling and covering their faces as I pointed at a flat noodle soup on a laminated menu affixed to the counter.

Foreign tourists must be thin on the ground in Hohhot, I thought as I carried my bowl over to a little table by the window.

Inner Mongolia was one of the few places that Lonely Planet almost discouraged people from visiting: 'Just how much you can see of the Mongolian way of life in China is dubious.' But I was still keen to see what I could.

I ate slowly, enjoying each fatty morsel of mutton. I was pretty good with chopsticks by that point – I'd never be a natural, but I didn't drop any bits of mutton into the soup with a splash, as I used to in Vietnam.

Hohhot seemed a scruffy, rather bleak sort of city – or at least in the area where I was staying close to the train station. Street vendors stood cheek by jowl on one side of the road, calling out the prices of their wares. The opposite side was under construction and the one still in use was unpaved, which meant that two lanes of traffic had to navigate a narrow area of bumpy stones while avoiding massive potholes and piles of dirt. I saw a motorbike and a three-wheel truck almost collide.

I spent the next few hours wandering around the Inner Mongolia Museum, which has a staggering collection of 44,000 items. Some of the best fossils in the world have been discovered in Inner Mongolia because its frozen tundra preserves them so effectively. The standout exhibit for me was the mammoth. It had been discovered in a coal mine in 1984 and most of its skeleton was the original bones rather than replicas. I gazed up at the enormous creature and tried to imagine it roaming the earth over a million years ago. Mind-boggling.

I admired the black-and-white portraits of Mongolian tribesmen, and then took photos of a big bronze statue of Genghis Khan astride his galloping mount. The founding leader of the Mongol Empire was the arch-nemesis of China, and parts of the Great Wall had been built with the express purpose of keeping out his marauding armies. Genghis Khan must have rolled in his grave when China seized control of a large swathe of his territory in 1947.

What was once Mongolia proper became a Chinese province known as 'Inner Mongolia Autonomous Region'. This long-winded name is an example of Orwellian double-speak. So-called 'Inner Mongolia' is part of China, whereas the independent country to the north is by inference 'Outer Mongolia'. Nor is the Chinese region autonomous. The Chinese state has forced Mongolians to assimilate. Their nomadic lifestyle and Buddhist beliefs had been pretty much eradicated, and although speaking Mongolian wasn't outlawed, learning the state language of Mandarin was non-negotiable.

On top of this, the government provided tax breaks and other financial incentives to China's majority ethnic group, the Han Chinese, if they relocated to Inner Mongolia. Mongolians now account for just one in five people among a total population of 24 million. The same policies of ethnic 'dilution' exist in China's four other 'autonomous regions', which include Tibet and Xinjiang, which is the home of the Uyghurs.

Shortly before I left the museum, I came to a plaque that described the official version of history, which was at odds with everything I'd read in my Lonely Planet.

'Since the founding of Inner Mongolia Autonomous Region

fifty years ago, a great change has happened on the grasslands, which is both a great victory of the minority policy and the result of the splendid leadership of the Communist Party of China. The people of all nationalities on the grassland will never forget the kind-hearted concerns of the revolutionary leaders of both the old and new generations.'

I rolled my eyes, snapped a photo of the plaque for posterity, and continued walking.

I DIDN'T VENTURE FAR from my hotel for dinner because I planned on having an early night. I chose a bustling restaurant with lots of families inside and was waiting for a waiter to come and start trying to guess my order when a group of men at the next table caught my eye. They seemed to be waving me over.

Me? I asked by pointing at myself.

Yes, they were nodding. *Shi de.*

I happily joined the group and introduced myself by saying that I was from 'Aodàlìyǎ'. I think they were Han Chinese, as they didn't look Mongolian. I whipped out my phrasebook and tried to say I had come from Beijing, but I was fairly certain they didn't understand me.

Anyhow, no matter. Ten shot glasses were filled from a huge bottle of baijiu, and I was soon laughing as if I was with old friends. One of the slightly older guys used a set of tongs to place wafer-thin slices of fatty pork into the bubbling hotpot on the table, followed by shiitake mushrooms and leafy greens. As the impromptu guest of honour, my bowl was filled first once it was cooked – by which time I'd already had three shots.

The hotpot was fantastic, and I had to remind myself not to finish everything in my bowl. Bethan had told me that Chinese etiquette requires a small amount of food not to be eaten at each meal. This indicates that it was so satisfying that it wasn't necessary to eat every last bite. As a kid, it was ingrained in me to finish everything on my plate. I loved food and was generally in the habit of licking my bowl clean, so I had to exercise a certain amount of restraint.

I had just rested my chopsticks across the top of my bowl to signal I was finished when I was invited to go sit on the wives' table, which was across from the men's. The women were very sweet and a couple of them seemed to be around my age. I once again tried to communicate using my phrasebook, but I was hopelessly drunk by then. I could hardly string a sentence together in English, let alone Mandarin. I was also beginning to feel queasy from the baijiu, so I gratefully accepted a cup of green tea from the porcelain teapot that came my way on the lazy Susan. After taking some photos together, I bid the two groups 'zaijian' (goodnight). I tried to contribute some yuan for the meal, but they wouldn't hear of it. I curtsied as a stupid sort of thank-you, and then I was on my way.

MORE HARD LIQUOR awaited me the following day. A striking woman in a red brocade gown with long sleeves handed me a small glass of baijiu as I stepped off the minibus a bit before noon.

'It's a tradition,' she said with a smile, while holding a tray full of shots.

I downed the baijiu with my backpack on and grinned as the backpacker behind me did the same. There were four foreign tourists on the tour, and about eight domestic ones. The liquor gave me an instant buzz, which I needed. I hadn't slept well and woke up feeling lousy, so I'd kept to myself during the two-hour journey. Even though I should have been excited, I got grumpier and grumpier as the reality of being on a tour began to sink in. Plus the landscape was not the verdant green steppes I'd been expecting. At this time of year, it was bone dry and dusty. It hadn't occurred to me to check whether my visit coincided with the low season.

I began chatting to the other tourists. The guy who had the baijiu after me was Lars from Holland. There was also a couple from Germany. I could immediately tell they were pretty strait-laced. Their clothes looked very clean and functional, and the girl refused the baijiu.

The woman in red introduced herself as Li, our tour guide. Then she led us along a path lined with spinifex to a dozen gers. They faced each other in a circle, and off to the right was a much larger ger with the evil eye painted on its roof and Tibetan prayer flags fluttering in the fierce winds. There were no other buildings in sight and no trees.

Li told us to meet inside the big ger in fifteen minutes after we'd put our stuff in the smaller gers she proceeded to assign us. Lars and I would be spending the night in a ger with '82' painted on its rusted red door. There certainly weren't eighty gers, so the logic behind the numbering system wasn't clear – but no matter. The German couple took the ger to the right of ours.

These were not portable tents for nomads. Each ger was mounted on a concrete base and I think the actual structure was made of concrete too, and merely wrapped in grey tarpaulins. The door was made of metal and at the top was a sort of chimney structure – perhaps for ventilation. Like igloos, the only opening was the door, and it was pitch-black inside. I located a dangling light switch as I entered.

'Ah – I love it!' I exclaimed.

It was a simple set-up, with single beds lining the perimeter and a low table in the middle of the room. Patterned sheets were draped from the concave ceiling. I chose the bed with a framed portrait of Genghis Khan above it. Lars put his backpack next to a bed on the other side. I was happy enough to share a ger with him. He gave off zero sleazy vibes.

'I might just take a couple of those extra blankets,' I said to Lars as I piled on a few extra floral quilts from another bed. The wind had an extra iciness to it out on the steppes and I shuddered to think what the temperature would drop to overnight. We zipped our jackets back up and headed out.

I wandered over to the toilet block, which was quite a distance from the gers. I made a mental note to drink as little as possible before getting into bed to avoid having to go in the night. Once I got closer to the toilets, I was glad they were so far away. The stench was unbelievable.

In the female section were two concrete stalls without doors. In the middle of the floor in each was a rectangular gap. I almost gagged. Just a few centimetres away from the concrete was an enormous pile of shit. I could make out bits of used toilet paper and sanitary pads and there were loads of flies buzzing around. Without running water or pipes, the excrement just sat there, day after day, building up. I would have turned and walked straight back out but I was busting for a wee. I held my breath so I wasn't inhaling the smells. I wanted to close my eyes too, but I was terrified of falling in, so I had to look at what I was doing. I couldn't get out of there fast enough.

'Oh my god, Lars – the drop toilets are totally disgusting,' I said after I met up with him in the big ger. 'It's just a pit of shit without running water.'

'I know an American girl who fell into a drop toilet in China last year,' he said.

'No way,' I said with a shudder.

'Yeah. She said it was terrible. She was in a really poor village somewhere in central China and she went to the toilet at night. She couldn't see that some of the wooden planks had gaps in them – and then one of them broke and she fell in. She was up to her neck in shit. She was screaming for people to come help her. Apparently it took them half an hour to fish her out, and all the while she could feel creatures writhing around her body. She cut her trip short and had to get counselling when she got home.'

'I bet she did,' I said. 'That's the most disgusting thing I've ever heard in my life. The poor girl.'

Just then Li appeared and said we were heading outside to watch horse racing and traditional wrestling after some sweet biscuits and tea. We assembled around a fenced area where there were about thirty ponies tethered to poles. Some were lying down while still saddled.

'Horses usually sleep while standing up, so these ponies must be knackered – pardon the pun,' I joked to Lars.

Notwithstanding, they looked to be in reasonably good condition, with shiny coats and no protruding ribs. There were chestnuts, bays and dapple greys.

I heard the sound of hoofbeats and looked behind me. A group of men on horseback came thundering across the steppes. It was a magnificent sight, and any lingering resentment I had about being on a tour melted away.

One of the men rode ahead of the rest. He was wearing a cobalt-blue brocaded tunic and his wavy black hair came down past his ears. He was really good-looking. He approached Li with a smile, said something to her and dismounted with the ease of someone who had probably started riding horses before he learned to walk. Li and the man exchanged a few words – I definitely saw her blush – and then he got back on.

'Gah!' he yelled as he dug his heels into his horse's sides.

The other horsemen followed after him with whoops, leaving a trail of dust in their wake. These Mongolian ponies were only about twelve or thirteen hands, but they sure were fast and could turn on a dime. I loved watching them carve up the dry earth.

Next a group of men on motorcycles appeared along the track. There were quite a lot of them – at least twenty. We formed a big circle and the traditional wrestling began. I wasn't sure what the rules were, but it was fairly self-explanatory: one man got another in a headlock and thumped him to the ground. The next man came along and fought the winner, and so on and so forth. The spectators egged on the fighters with what I assumed were good natured cat calls. Everyone was grinning. By the time the wrestling matches were over, the fighters were absolutely covered in dust and the sun was beginning to set. I'm sure it was all staged for our benefit, but it was good fun.

With the seamless orchestration of a tour that has been done a thousand times before, we gravitated to the big ger. Dinner was bubbling away in a large clay pot and it smelled pretty good. There was also a big vat of noodles with black sauce and the ubiquitous Chinese vegetables of thinly sliced carrot, bok choy, baby corn and onion. There was a bottle of baijiu on each table.

We were serenaded with traditional music while we ate. One of the instruments reminded me of the didgeridoo and there was also a violin. I had read that strands of horse mane are used to make violin strings. The male singer had a deep voice that was almost a warble, and it was hauntingly beautiful.

Five men and women emerged from behind a red curtain and began to dance. They wore long-sleeved, billowing satin tunics that were cinched at the waist with embroidered belts. One of the women had a tall hat made of white beads that dangled down to her waist. It must have been heavy. It was a high-energy display of kicks and splits and parts of it were reminiscent of Irish dancing. They twirled their billowing skirts like sufis. The Chinese tourists started clapping in time with the music and then we all joined in. Sure, it was a bit cheesy, but I was really enjoying myself. At the end of the concert we had photos with the performers as they were still trying to catch their breath.

We were given torches to light our way back to our gers. It was absolutely freezing, so I wore all my clothes to bed. I snuggled into my blankets and pulled them right up to my chin, feeling grateful for the warmth of Bethan's jumper.

Mercifully, I slept right through until morning and avoided a late-night visit to the shit pit.

When I wandered out of the ger the next morning, breakfast was being prepared nearby. The carcass of a freshly slaughtered sheep was hanging from the back of a trailer. A man was skinning it while the blood drained out of its neck into a big metal bowl. Its head was in a second bowl, while squares of wool were laid out flat to dry on a tarp. A toddler in a puffy orange jacket was playing in the dust while his mother worked away at skinning parts of the wool. What distressed me more than butchery up close was the live sheep that was watching on from the back of the trailer. He presumably knew he was next.

After a breakfast of 'sheep stomach stew with assorted tendons' (as Li described it) we headed out for a ride on the steppes. I couldn't wait to ride a horse again. I'd spent most of my childhood obsessed with horses, and I was lucky enough to have one for a few years, until I got older and became more interested in hockey and parties.

I rode a stocky bay with a trimmed mane that bobbed up and down as it trotted along the path. I looked over its perky little ears. The saddle had an uncomfortable pommel that kept jabbing me in the stomach, but I loved being under the wide open sky. It was a pale blue with just a few wispy clouds. Sheep grazed and crows rested on clumps of rocky outcrops.

I winced at the Chinese guy ahead of me, who was bouncing out of time to the rhythm of his horse's gait and landing with a heavy bump in the saddle; his oversized suit flapping in the wind and his feet poking out straight in the stirrups. Much easier on the eye was the guide two horses ahead of him. He was every inch the Mongolian cowboy. Dressed from head to toe in black, he wore a leather jacket, cowboy hat and scuffed black cowboy boots. He never took off his wraparound sunglasses and he spoke little. He smouldered like the heartthrob actor, Patrick Swayze.

We'd travelled several kilometres when we came to a building block that was the same greyish brown as the earth. Inside it had a cottage feel. We sat around a table covered with a frilly tablecloth and drank yak milk. As we did, Lars told me about his day trip to North Korea. While in South Korea for a couple of weeks, he had visited the demilitarised zone (better known as the 'DMZ'), where a ceasefire was negotiated between the two Koreas in 1953. In a military building is what is known as the 'demarcation line' – and Lars had one foot in North Korea and another in South Korea. I hung on his every word.

Our conversation got me thinking about how cool it would be to go to North Korea. I was actually quite close to the border. When I got back to the ger, I retrieved my Lonely Planet out of my bag and thumbed to the section titled 'Getting there and away', which had instructions for every country that borders China.

'Visas are difficult to arrange to North Korea and at the time of writing, it was virtually impossible for US and South Korean citizens. Those interested in travelling to North Korea from Beijing should get in touch with Koryo Tours, who can get you there (and back).'

I was pretty sure the cost would be prohibitive for my budget and decided to stick with my existing plan of cutting south-west towards Tibet. Maybe one day I'd get the chance to visit North Korea, but it wouldn't be on this trip.

Once back in Hohhot, I boarded a train bound for Pingyao. As I watched the apartment blocks pass by in a blur, I thought with satisfaction about the past twenty-four hours. Any visit to Inner Mongolia is problematic, but I couldn't fault the Chinese tour company. They had made every effort to keep us entertained. Mongolian culture was so new to me that I couldn't even tell whether something was authentic or staged, but I had seen and done all the things I hoped to during my visit. And, sure, my time there was really brief. But I'd be forever grateful to have seen a part of the world I thought I'd only ever get to see in a documentary.

21

TROUBLE IN PARADISE

I spent the final hour of the flight from Xi'an to Tibet with my face pressed against the window. We passed over undulating ridges that looked like crumpled velvet and snow-capped peaks that poked through the clouds like stiff egg whites. The vast Himalayan mountain range is the highest on the planet, which is why Tibet is known as 'the Roof of the World'.

As we neared the capital city of Lhasa, a patchwork of irrigated fields came into sight, along with farmhouses, roads and monasteries. A stunning turquoise river and its tributaries were sandwiched by a vast expanse of sandy-grey sediment. It almost looked as though landlocked Tibet had a beach.

The small aircraft began its descent and landed with just a few wobbles and bumps. With an elevation of 3700 metres, Lhasa is one of the highest cities in the world. When I'd bought my flight and travel permit a few days earlier, the travel agent had told me that flights always left first thing in the morning because strong air currents pick up in the afternoon. She also said pilots had to be specially trained to manoeuvre the high-altitude landing in Tibet's thin air.

When we disembarked straight onto the tarmac, I asked a Chinese tourist to take my photo. I grinned and raised my hand triumphantly. I had made it to Tibet!

However, my excitement was tempered with apprehension because I was worried about getting altitude sickness. The chances of that were quite high (pardon the pun) by virtue of arriving in Tibet by plane. My body would have a difficult time adjusting to the sudden increase in altitude, which brought with it decreased oxygen levels and low air pressure. A gradual ascent by train would have been preferable, but after eight days in Pingyao and Xi'an, I was running out of time on my already extended Chinese visa, and I needed to factor in another week for the journey from Lhasa to Nepal.

I retrieved my pack from the conveyer belt and headed to a cab rank while focusing on my breathing. Was it short and rapid? My mind was going to have a field day playing tricks on me. Other early symptoms to look out for included headaches, nausea, fatigue and loss of appetite. If altitude sickness was going to strike, it would most likely occur in the next six to twenty-four hours. I planned to stay in Lhasa for a few days before moving on to a place with a higher altitude. There were no rescue facilities in Tibet, so it was important to do all I could to prevent the life-threatening illness. All I had by way of medicines to treat altitude sickness was the Diamox tablets and Chinese traditional medicine I'd brought with me.

When I checked into Snowland Hotel, I could see why my guidebook described it as having seen better days. The three-storey white, stucco building was in need of a spruce up, with its once pretty window frames either rusted or busted. Apparently it also had unreliable hot-water supplies – which is no small inconvenience when temperatures regularly drop below freezing. Apparently Snowland Hotel had become the least popular option in town for budget travellers, but options remained limited.

I wasn't deterred by the less-than-enthusiastic review because I wanted to stay in a dormitory. If I got altitude sickness, I didn't want to be alone in a hotel room with breathing difficulties. I was relieved to be told there was a free bed in the ten-person dormitory and thought how in the past I'd done all I could to avoid a shared room.

The dorm had the feel of a classroom, with large windows on both sides and curling, yellowed posters of local landmarks like Jokhang Temple and the Potala Palace. The top half of the wallpaper was decorated with a pretty Tibetan motif, beneath which were thick stripes of pale pink and mint green. Two rows of single beds were divided by an aisle that had a few tables for storing travellers' belongings. There were utensils, mugs, packets of noodles and dry biscuits. Damp towels were draped across the spindly table legs.

Only about half the beds were taken. I put down my pack at the foot of a bed near the door. There was nowhere else to put it – the beds were so close they were practically touching. There were a couple of human-shaped lumps under the blankets – late sleepers, I figured. There was also a guy sitting on the bed across from mine. He was writing in his journal and he looked up and smiled at me. I smiled back, while crossing my fingers that he didn't snore.

The dorm was on the second floor, and it had an excellent vantage point of the street below. I could observe people going about their business without being noticed. I took out my camera and stayed there a while, enjoying as I did the pleasures of street photography. I clicked the shutter furiously as three women in dark woollen dresses and striped aprons came along carrying large sacks over their shoulders. They walked determinedly with their heads down. Their faces were obscured by white, wide-brimmed straw hats with big bows at the back, a type of formal ladies sunhat I associated with the 1920s. It was such an interesting aesthetic. I wondered what their lives were like.

It was a short walk to the Jokhang Temple from Snowland Hotel, so I headed there first as a way of getting my bearings. It is considered the most sacred of Tibetan temples because it has a particularly special statue of Buddha inside. First built in the seventh century, it features the distinctive Tibetan combination of white stucco, maroon trimming and gold flourishes, with rows of narrow windows adorned with crimped cream valences.

The public square facing the temple was a hive of activity, with a constant stream of Tibetans walking past, all in the same clockwise direction. Many were fondling prayer beads or carrying prayer wheels. The wheels were also spun in a clockwise direction, as it represents the movement of the sun across the sky. They were making a pilgrim circuit known as a 'kora'. The kilometre-long walk around the perimeter of the temple in Barkhor Square and other sacred spots is both a meditation and a prayer, and it was obvious they were deeply immersed in the ritual. One of the women that came past had braided hair interwoven with red yarn, and wore a chunky turquoise necklace that looked as heavy as a croquet ball. The man behind her wore a ragged sheepskin. There were also scores of monks in brown and burgundy robes. They bowed with their hands clasped in the prayer position, facing the temple. Other devotees were doing a series of motions that was a bit like a gentle burpee. The final part involved sliding along the ground on their stomachs. Many had blocks of wood tied to their palms to protect them against the cobblestones. Their foreheads touched the ground for a couple of heartbeats before they leaped to their feet and repeated the prostration.

Two totem poles were wrapped loosely with Tibetan prayer

flags and black wool, while a huge incense burner that looked like a pot belly stove was tended by a monk. As I stood there watching the comings and goings, a little girl came up to me and asked me for money. She couldn't have been more than five. Her black hair was in tiny plaits and she wore a bright-green tunic over an embroidered woollen skirt. She smiled at me impishly, holding out a wad of yuan and pleading for me to add to it. I found it impossible to refuse a child so young and gave her ten yuan. She let me take her photo and then she smiled and scampered off to count her earnings as she sat on a step in the sunshine.

Considering how remote Tibet is, I was surprised to see quite a lot more Western tourists than I'd expected. But perhaps I shouldn't have been surprised. Tibet is extraordinarily beautiful and it has had a hold on the Western imagination for centuries. The power of its mystique as a spiritual Shangri-la is difficult to quantify and its allure is further bolstered by its status as something of a hidden kingdom. It only opened up to tourism in the 1980s and it is periodically sealed off to foreign tourists for years at a time. Foreign journalists cannot get permits for Tibet. I also blamed Tibet's popularity on Brad Pitt. Like no doubt every other Western tourist who has travelled there, I'd oohed and aahed over the Hollywood blockbuster *Seven Years in Tibet*, which stars Pitt as an Austrian mountaineer who befriends the Dalai Lama as a young man during the Second World War.

Most of the Western tourists looked to be in their fifties and sixties on small packaged tours. It made sense that foreign tourists would be wealthier types. Tibet is poor, but it's an expensive place to travel to. Tours are mandatory outside of Lhasa, and separate permits are required for every destination and cost a couple of hundred dollars apiece.

Barkhor Square's market stalls clearly catered to Tibet's

tourism industry. There were souvenirs of every description, from block prints of holy scriptures to turquoise beaded jewellery and the ubiquitous prayer flags. There were colourful wooden masks of angry gods and Buddha heads that ranged in size from those that could fit in the palm of my hand to the garden-sized variety.

I had just bought a green pashmina when I felt a tugging on my back pocket. I spun around and saw a guy shrinking away before I had time to slap his hand. My eyes flashed with anger and he smiled back at me with contempt. I was too slow to think of what to do, and before I knew it he had darted into an alleyway. All he would have got was a bunch of snotty tissues, but it was the first time during my trip that anyone had tried to pickpocket me. I was so surprised that it had happened in Tibet, of all places.

Snowland Hotel had Lhasa's only public internet café, so I headed back there to see if there was a reply from Bert. I saw my email to him had bounced. With a sigh, I corrected the email address and resent it. I guess I'd be going out for dinner on my own that night.

Next I read an email from Dad. He sounded pretty sad and disappointed. I had finally told him and Mum that I wanted to teach English in South Korea after my year-long trip was over. I couldn't afford to fly to London to meet them and then fly back to Seoul, so if I decided to go ahead with this new plan, I wouldn't be able to see them in London. Dad wasn't angry. He said they had been excited about seeing me and he hoped that teaching English was the right step to take for my career. I could tell he thought it wasn't. I think he wished with all his heart that I would pursue a career in law. He signed off by asking if I could let him know within the next two weeks whether I would go to London; they needed to confirm their holiday with the travel agent. I left with my stomach tied up in knots.

As I washed down my yak curry with a couple of beers at a hole-in-the-wall eatery up the road, I went back and forth over different scenarios for my future. On the one hand, I wanted to pursue a life that would make me happy, and it was increasingly clear that working in an office in London would not achieve that. I'd be just as unfulfilled as I had been in Melbourne. On the other hand, my parents had done so much for me over the years. That included letting me move back home for a year rent-free so I could save up for my trip. I didn't want to disappoint them by not being in London as planned.

I wanted to see Bert because as a fellow backpacker, he was sure to understand my predicament, and would hopefully make me feel better. I wondered what his parents thought about him learning Tibetan for six months. It was not the most practical skill to acquire.

The dormitory was dark and freezing. I took off just my jacket and hopped inside my sleeping sheet. Then I layered a couple of thick blankets on top. Across the other side of the room was a backpacker reading a book with a light strapped to his forehead.

I was woken in the middle of the night by a loud scratching. I propped myself up on my elbows and tried to work out where it was coming from. A rat ran across the inside of the window ledge, its silhouette illuminated by the moonlight. An even bigger friend scampered along behind him. Gross. The snacks left out on the tables must be attracting them. I tucked my arms inside the sleeping bag sheet and went back to sleep.

I wasn't feeling so great when I woke up the next morning. I had a headache and my body was kind of tingly. True to form, the hot water in the shower ran out before I'd had time to get the shampoo out of my hair, so I shivered as I rinsed and dried myself.

When I came back to the dorm, I noticed another backpacker was groaning softly in bed. Another guy was sitting next to him, looking worried. I looked across at the guy on the bed next to mine, who was eating a muesli bar in his bed.

Not great for the rat situation, I thought.

'Does he need a doctor?' I said, alarmed.

'He's been sick for the past couple of days, but he is getting better now.'

'I'm scared I will get altitude sickness,' I confessed.

'Ah, I think you're more likely to get food poisoning. Almost every traveller I have met in Tibet has been sick with it. I just got better. Don't eat the street food. It's not hygienic.'

After the warning, Jakob told me he was from Norway. His other tip was to go up to the roof, as it had an amazing view. After climbing the two sets of stairs, I was almost wheezing. I was way more out of breath than usual.

I took some photographs of the magnificent view of snow-capped mountains, Tibetan prayer flags, a balcony filled with yellow daisies in pots and the Potala Palace in the distance. I basked in the warmth of the sun. It was a welcome relief that Lhasa was far warmer than I expected it to be during the daytime.

I was happy to read a reply from Bert. He was staying at Kirey Hotel and gave me his room number. He said he and Franziska could be found every night at Namsto Restaurant, because the Nepalese curries there were amazing. I jotted down the address and wrote back to say I'd see them there that evening.

With my headache dulled by paracetamol, I went back to the dorm to drop off my jumper and saw another two backpackers lying in bed unwell. One had a grey complexion and his eyes were closed. The other had a warm compresses on his forehead. I looked sympathetically at their friend sitting on the end of a bed. It was alarming that backpackers seemed to be dropping like flies.

I walked to Potala Palace at a gentle pace to avoid getting out of breath, and stopped along the way for a cup of yak butter tea at an outdoor tea stall. I wasn't expecting it to be salty and spluttered on the first sip. I couldn't finish it. The tea stall also had a display of yak butter and chunks of yak cheese, the latter of which was so pale it was practically white. Yaks were quite literally the backbone of agriculture in Tibet. Their wool was used for clothing, their milk and meat consumed, their dung burned for fuel and they were ridden and carried goods over mountainous terrain.

There was a noticeably higher population of Han Chinese in the commercial district of Lhasa, and there were quite a few department stores and a mall as well. It looked much like any nondescript Chinese city. The Chinese government provided economic incentives to Han Chinese for relocating to Tibet, just as it did for those who relocated to Inner Mongolia. This resulted in diluting the relative strength of Tibetans in Tibet, although the government touts the policy as promoting 'progress'.

I stopped from afar to take in the architectural masterpiece that is the Potala Palace, and kept taking more photographs as I got closer. Built onto a steep slope, the palace's sloping stone walls criss-cross up the mountainside. It almost felt as if I was looking at an optical illusion, as it was hard to determine whether its proportions were both vertical and horizontal. The top part of the 1000-bedroom palace is a block of maroon, while the lower parts are white. The massively wide steps and walls that descend to the bottom of the mountain look like cascading snow.

The Potala Palace had been the winter residence of the Dalai Lama since the seventh century, but after he fled to India in 1959 following the Chinese takeover of Tibet, it became a museum. Public openings are limited to certain days of the week, for one hour maximum, and bookings are required. I could only admire the palace from the outside.

An enormous Chinese flag flew right in the middle of the palace, while two red banners with gold Chinese characters ran all the way across the lower base of the wall. It was irritating that I couldn't get a photo of the beautiful palace without either the flag or the banner in the way. I was already noticing subtle and not so subtle reminders that Tibet is Chinese territory: the restaurant where I was meeting Bert and Franziska was on East Beijing Road, and the clocks in Tibet ran on Beijing time, even though it was thousands of kilometres away. This meant it got light just before 8 am and dark after 8 pm. According to my guidebook, Tibetans mostly ignored the official time and organised their days in line with the actual sunrise and sunset.

WHEN I WALKED into the restaurant, Bert stood up to give me a big hug and then introduced me to Franziska and their friends, Luca and Peter. I ordered a beer and a plate of momos soon arrived. I was really happy to be back with part of my Beijing group of friends.

Franziska was lovely. She had porcelain skin, green eyes and short, jet-black hair. She reminded me of Winona Ryder. She was doing her masters in Laos for the next five months, after which time she and Bert would head back home to Leipzig in Germany. It was fun to reminisce about the places I'd travelled to in Laos, and it was so nice to have female company. Franziska gave me some of her tea tree oil to treat my sunburnt nose after I laughed and told her I'd learned the hard way that Tibet is much closer to the sun. My nose was so red I looked like a clown.

Bert asked me how I liked Tibet so far. I said that I liked it very much, although there was a clear undercurrent of tension and more poverty than I'd expected. I mentioned I had almost been robbed the day before, and it was hard not to feel a bit on edge.

'I'm sorry to hear that,' said Luca sympathetically. 'Something bad happened to me too, just this morning. A monk demanded money from me out the front of Potala Palace. When I said no, he scratched me.'

'A monk scratched you?' I asked, incredulous.

'You would not believe it, huh.'

'Maybe it wasn't a real monk,' said Bert, which bewildered me even more.

'Tibet is beautiful, but troubled,' added Franziska thoughtfully.

I nodded in agreement and took another sip of beer. I'd expected Tibetans to be serene and peace-loving, but I'd realised this was a bit idealistic. For one, Tibetans had spent decades fighting a resistance against Chinese occupation. Many Tibetans belonged to warrior tribes. The best known were the Khampa warriors, who led the resistance movement using mostly guerrilla tactics. They are famous within the region for being volatile and fierce. It was a Khampa tribesman who protected the Dalai Lama when he fled to India in 1959.

My guidebook summed it up like this: 'Tibetans have never had it easy. Their environment is harsh, and human habitation has always been a precarious proposition. By necessity, Tibetans have become a tough and resilient people.'

Bert changed the subject by saying that he, Franziska and Luca were planning a trip that weekend to Samye Monastery. It was a couple of hours from Lhasa and the altitude was more or less the same. It is Tibet's oldest monastery and I really wanted to go, but I didn't think I could afford it. The mandatory tours were pricey.

'We're not going on a tour,' said Bert. 'Travelling independently will save us a couple of hundred dollars.'

'What if we get caught? I thought tourists weren't even allowed to travel on public transport?'

'Well, that's true. If we get caught, we'll get a big fine. But we've met quite a few people at Kirey Hotel who travelled there just last week without getting caught.'

'We will just keep a low profile on the bus there,' added Franziska. 'Wear a pashmina and wrap it over your hair.'

'All right then,' I said, although I wasn't as cavalier about it as I may have sounded. 'I'm in.'

We headed off to a folk music bar and met up with a Tibetan guy called Renchin who was giving Bert informal Tibetan lessons before he began studying at a local centre. The bar was in a basement, with sandstone walls and oak furniture. The girls behind the bar were very friendly, if not forthright in the way they came up to Bert and bear-hugged him. The performers on the little stage had bellowing, guttural voices that were a bit similar to what I'd seen in Inner Mongolia. When a set ended, I asked Renchin what he thought about us sneaking off to Samye Monastery.

'I think it's unfair that the Chinese government gets paid every time a tourist visits Tibet,' he said, with more than a trace of bitterness in his voice.

By the time I was walking back to the dorm at Snowland Hotel it was after 11 pm. I passed two enormous carcasses of yaks. One was on a truck and another was on a tarpaulin, out the back of a shop. It was absolutely freezing, so there was no question the meat would be affected by being handled in the open air. I immediately thought of the mammoth in the museum.

I was halfway home when I decided to snack on a tangerine. I'd bought a bag from a street hawker earlier in the day. I figured an extra dose of Vitamin C would help ease the cold I could feel coming on. I started to peel a piece of fruit as I walked. A group of street kids stepped out of the shadows of the alley.

'Give us some,' said a boy roughly.

I thought about it and grudgingly agreed. They were only kids, but something told me to avoid getting into a situation with them. Without saying thank you, they took off with the fruit and erupted into peals of laughter.

What are kids doing out at eleven o'clock at night anyway? I thought grumpily as I continued walking.

~

I SLIPPED into the seat next to Franziska. The bus pulled out of the station at Barkhor Square while it was still dark, which made it easier for us to hop on without being asked any questions. Bert and Luca were sitting in front of us with their beanies pulled down. The four of us sat quietly on the back seats and made it to Chimpu Valley undetected a couple of hours later.

We wandered into the grounds of the monastery and were greeted by the friendly guesthouse manager. We told him straight up that we had come without permits.

'You'll be fine,' he said. 'It's very remote here. And, anyway, it's a stupid system. Why should the Chinese government make money out of you coming to stay at my guesthouse?'

He led us to a big room with four single beds and then we wandered around the monastery grounds. It was a beautiful monastery in a secluded setting, with steep mountains all around. It is laid out in the shape of a giant mandala, which is a circular figure that represents the universe in Buddhist thought. At the entrance was a large bronze bell, and in the centre was the main temple representing the legendary Mount Meru. Other buildings stood at the corners and cardinal points of the main temple, representing continents and other features of tantric Buddhist cosmology. There were quite a lot of monks about, but we didn't see any other tourists. It felt pretty special to be there, although I wasn't quite sure how we would fill the rest of the day.

The guys had a nap and Franziska and I talked some more. As the sun began to set we played cards. At dusk we went to the restaurant for yak stew. We returned to our room and cracked open a bottle of rum, which I drank to give me warmth as much as anything else. My nose was really blocked from the cold and our room had no insulation from the elements. With half the bottle emptied, Luca began to pretend he was a member of the Chinese police force. I leaped to my feet and guarded the door as if I was James Bond holding a pistol. We laughed our heads off and were asleep by nine o'clock.

We had just stepped out of our room in the morning when we almost collided with the guesthouse manager, who came bounding along the path. I could tell from the look on his face that something was wrong.

'The PSB are here,' he said, referring to the police force officially known as the Public Security Bureau. 'They are checking our facilities and tourist permits. Go to the roof and stay there until I tell you it's safe to come down.'

We made a beeline for the stairs. My heart was thumping in my chest. We could hear the two police officers knocking on the doors of each room below. Two staff members came up to the roof carrying our packs. There was no shade on the roof and the sun was beating down on us. After an hour, we began to bicker.

'We can't stay here forever,' said Luca. 'Surely we can go back to our room now they've checked them.'

'Luca, the fine is over three hundred dollars,' said Bert. 'They might even kick me out of Tibet and I'm meant to be here for five more months. We need to wait here until the manager tells us it is safe to leave.'

'Well, I think the PSB will check the roof,' said Luca grumpily.

I saw Bert squeeze Franziska's hand. She had stayed quiet throughout and she looked really worried.

'How long do you think they will hang around for?' I asked.

The manager came up then and quietly told us to follow him down the stairs. We ran along a path and out the back of the monastery. There was a gap in the mud fence that we leaped over. There was a minibus waiting for us with the engine on. We waved goodbye to the guesthouse manager. What a kind guy. I was sorry to have caused him stress on our behalf.

The minibus dropped us at a boat ramp, where a speedboat was waiting at the edge of Lake Namsto. Other passengers were already onboard, including an old lady with microbraids down to her thighs. We were soon speeding across the highest lake in the world, whose waters were a brilliant topaz colour. If ever I felt as if I was in a James Bond movie, it was at that moment.

Anne Reid with Jack and Isabella at Amigo Mansion in Happy Valley, Hong Kong.

Beautiful Yangshuo in southern China.

Jess and Mei-Xing having hotpot in Guilin, China.

Jess with cousins Isabella, Jack and Philip Reid at the Hong Kong Football Club.

Sampling Chinese teas in Shanghai with Clem and Russell.

Josiah, Bruce, Phil, Yvonne and Jess at the Great Wall of China.

At the Great Wall of China

The head of the Mongolian horsemen I saw during my whirlwind tour of the grassland steppes.

Samye Monastery, Tibet.

A Tibetan woman selling prayer flags near the base camp of Mount Everest.

Coming down from Mount Everest Basecamp in a horse and cart.

Jess at Mount Everest in Tibet.

22

SKY HIGH

Once safely back in Lhasa, I met up with Bert and Franziska at Summit Café. Bert had declared its coffee the best in town, and there were certainly loads of travellers hanging out there that morning.

I still had a cold that I couldn't seem to shake, but I was otherwise unaffected by altitude sickness. I felt confident enough to travel to a higher altitude. A much higher altitude, in fact. I'd been seized by the idea of going to Everest Base Camp, which has an altitude of 5200 metres. The trouble was that the expedition cost several hundred dollars. If I spent that kind of money, I'd have to cut my trip short by two or three weeks. Trying to decide what to do was agony. Surely it was a once-in-a-lifetime opportunity. When would I ever be this close to the world's tallest mountain again?

'You never know how life will turn out,' said Bert, stirring a sugar into his espresso. 'Maybe you'll get the chance to come back to Tibet in a few years.'

'I don't think the chances of that are very high,' I said glumly.

Just then a middle-aged woman in hiking gear approached our table.

'I'm sorry to interrupt,' she said with a smile. 'But I overheard you saying just now how much you'd like to go to Mount Everest. I actually have a spare seat in a jeep that's leaving tomorrow, because one of the people who was meant to come with us has fallen sick. From Mount Everest, we will continue on to Kathmandu. It will take about a week. If you don't mind sitting in the very back seat with the bags and gear, you can pay us half the going rate. How does that sound?'

'I would love that!' I exclaimed. 'Thank you so much.'

'Great,' she said. 'I'm Lynne.'

'I'm Jess.'

'Here's a business card with my hotel's address. We're leaving from the hotel carpark at 5 am tomorrow. See you there, okay? And please bring the cash to pay upfront.'

'You bet I'll see you there,' I said. 'I'll go to a bank right away.'

I sat there in a daze for a few seconds, unable to believe my luck. Then I hugged Bert and Franziska goodbye and jogged back to Snowland Hotel so I could send an email to Mum and Dad about my exciting news.

I got sidetracked when I walked into the hotel's courtyard and saw a massive yellow truck. A small group of people had crowded around a man who was lying on a blanket next to the vehicle. He had on an oxygen mask. I asked one of the girls in the group if he was okay, and she said he'd woken up complaining of breathing difficulties and they'd come down from a higher altitude right away. In a worried voice, she told me the group was travelling in the truck from Istanbul to Bangkok. I realised then that the back of the truck had been converted into about twenty bench seats.

I told her I hoped he got better soon, and headed into the internet café. It was scary to see someone so sick with altitude sickness, but it didn't make me reconsider my plans. The opportunity was just too good to miss. But I certainly didn't mention the sick traveller to Mum and Dad when I told them I was about to head off on a week-long expedition to Mount Everest. Instead, I joked with typical bravado that I was going to hoist the Mudditt flag at base camp. I signed off by promising to give them a firm decision about my post-travelling plans once I had made it to Nepal.

While at the computer, I was chuffed to read a lovely email from Paula from my Vietnam leg. She said she really enjoyed reading my group emails and even encouraged me to turn them into a book one day. She was such a kind and encouraging person.

I'M glad you liked the email – maybe I will do something with them one day,' I replied. *'But so many people write great travel stuff; it's a pretty well-covered market. I really appreciate the compliment though!*

AFTER A FITFUL LAST sleep in the dormitory, I snuck out at 4:30 am. At the hotel carpark I met Lynne and gave her the money. She introduced me to her partner, Louise, and the other three people on the expedition. There was a British man, Paul, an Israeli girl called Schlomi, and a Tibetan driver called Champa. Once Champa had put our packs inside the jeep, I hopped into the backseat of the seven seater. It was a bit squishy, but I considered my spot a golden ticket.

It would take us three days to reach the drop-off point for base camp. Lynne said we would take it slowly and make strategic stops at rest houses that were lower than the altitude we had reached during the day. Each day, we'd travel a little higher.

The five of us had a chat over lunch at a tavern in a dusty town. Lynne and Louise were lawyers at big firms in London. They'd been dreaming of going to Mount Everest for years. Paul had written several books on archeology and this trip was part of his research for a new one. Schlomi didn't really explain why she was in Tibet. She didn't say much, other than to explain that she was an Orthodox Jew and only ate kosher food. She didn't have any of the chow-mien and instead stuck to fruit and trail mix. I was bowled over by her commitment. I had been eating like a scavenger in China.

It was a long day, so I felt tired when we pulled up at a rest house for the night. Schlomi and I put our stuff together in a small room that had no furniture other than three single beds. She brought out her camping stove to cook her dinner and I said I'd keep her company. As she chopped up some vegetables, I asked her what brought her to Tibet. I was surprised by her response. She told me her fiancé had recently called off their engagement just days before the wedding. She was heartbroken and humiliated. With sorrow in her eyes, she told me she got on a plane to the furthest place she could think of from home.

'Since I was a kid, I was always fascinated by the Himalayas,' she added.

I felt so sorry for her.

We went to bed early and were awoken around midnight. I heard a guy's voice, half whispering something in Tibetan. Then he started half laughing, half shouting. There was banging on the windows. I was grateful to know there were bars on them. Then the door started rattling.

'Jess! Jess!'

Schlomi leaped across the dark room and sat next to me. There were at least two guys out there and they were louder now. They were banging on the door. We had to think fast.

'Let's push the third bed in front of the door,' I said.

'Good idea.'

We hauled it over and then went back to our beds. Neither of us slept. I was deeply unnerved, and also pissed off.

We told Lynne and Louise what had happened – that maybe they were drunk local guys. The other women just kind of brushed us off, as though we'd told them an amusing tale. I wasn't sure if they had misunderstood, but whatever. It wasn't as though their sympathy would change what had happened. Schlomi and I were glad to leave that town.

Early the next afternoon, we stopped at the second-largest city in Tibet, Shigatse. On the top of a hillcrest was a stunning monastery that looked just like the Potala Palace. Champa said it was a good place to buy a cheap but very thick jumper. Out the front of a small shopping mall was a group of girls on their way back from school. They came over and said hi to me in Tibetan. We couldn't understand each other, but they led me to a nearby public garden where we mucked around taking photos of each other with my camera. One of the girls was so beautiful, and had purple yarn entwined in the plaits that framed her forehead. She was also really mischievous.

Lynne snapped at me when I got back to the rest house. Apparently I hadn't told her that I was going to the shops and she'd been worried.

Weird way to show your concern, I thought huffily.

Bleary-eyed, we hopped back in the jeep at dawn and continued along the Friendship Highway. Its name was ironic, given how poorly our group was getting along. Lynne and Louise kept squabbling with each other, Paul and Champa were men of few words, and Schlomi radiated sadness. My attempt to liven the mood with some banter had fallen flat. They were super straight. I kept my eye on the prize: just one more day and I'd be climbing Mount Everest.

At times the landscape was so stark it resembled a moon

crater. We saw no signs of life for miles. Even on this remote, circuitous highway, there were reminders of Chinese occupation. Every few hundred metres was a concrete boulder stating how many kilometres we were from Beijing. I saw a monastery plonked on top of a steep mountain, with nothing whatsoever for miles. The hardiness of the Tibetan people was extraordinary. It was a mystery to me as to how the monastery was built, and how people managed to live there.

We stopped at a tiny village to use the facilities. The half a dozen houses were built with slabs of grey stone and the front doorway was a curtain cut in two. Paul pointed out a couple of homes made of yak dung. I didn't see a single person out and about, and wondered if they were shepherds.

And then the day of the climb arrived. We made it to Rongbuk Monastery just after 8 am. It is just eight kilometres from Everest Base Camp. Needless to say, it is the highest monastery in the world.

Champa stopped the jeep a few hundred metres away so we could take photographs at a viewing area, which was marked by a pile of stones, a yak skull and some prayer flags. A few Tibetan women were there, rugged up and selling trinkets. I bought some prayer flags and then began to take photos.

The north face of the mountain was immediately recognisable to me, as I had stared at it in my guidebook so many times. But now here it was, in all its majestic beauty, and I was taking photographs of what was perhaps the greatest natural world wonder.

I felt a drip on my chin and put my hand to my nose. I had a nosebleed. I wasn't sure if it was caused by the cold or the altitude, or both.

I am so far off course from the Chase the Sun Tour, I thought as I dabbed it with tissues.

The four of us set out. Champa remained with the jeep at

the monastery, which also had a guesthouse. The path was wide and mostly free of snow, so it wasn't difficult terrain. But I was flagging. My whole body felt like lead and each step was an effort. But I forgot all that when we came across a glacier. It was really beautiful, but I stayed well back. The thought of slipping and falling to my death terrified me.

On we went. After an hour or so, I heard the clip clopping of hooves and saw a horse and cart coming towards us.

'Kris! Roland!' exclaimed Lynne as the cart drew level with us.

'Oh wow – hi Lynne,' replied one of the two men sitting behind the Tibetan cart driver. 'How funny to see you again, and here, of all places.'

'Isn't it just. A small world, eh. Are you returning from base camp?'

'We are, yes,' said the guy with an olive complexion. 'We made it to base camp two, and we stayed there overnight. The view at dawn was incredible. Freezing though,' he added with a laugh.

'My camera froze up, unfortunately,' said the blond, holding up an impressive-looking SLR camera.

I stood there listening, open-mouthed. I'd been told the trek to that spot was incredibly difficult and dangerous.

'Hello,' the blond-haired guy suddenly said to me.

'This is Jess,' said Lynne. 'And Paul and Schlomi. This is Kris and Roland.'

'Hi, Jess,' said Kris.

'Hello,' I said, suddenly shy.

'Good luck with the rest of your trek,' he said, still smiling at me. 'Enjoy the view.'

I smiled and nodded, and then the driver cracked the reins and the pony took off down the mountain at a trot.

Wow. What a pair of gorgeously, rugged, tough men.

I tried to casually ask Lynne for some information about them. Kris was Dutch and Roland was Russian. Coincidentally, they'd travelled together from Nepal into Tibet, where they stayed for a couple of weeks before returning to Nepal. That was all Lynne said and I didn't want to seem weird by asking if she knew anything else.

On we went. The sun was out and I walked along thinking how extraordinary it was that I was hiking to Mount Everest. Never in my wildest dreams did I imagine I'd have such an adventure.

I was jubilant when we reached base camp. Mount Everest was so close, and it was incredibly beautiful. A Tibetan woman approached our group and showed us inside a tent, where we could stay that night if we wanted to. A little sign out the front said its name was Hotel California. Another sign advertised hot chocolate. It blew me away that she worked here, day in and day out.

Strong winds were whipping at the tent. It was about minus two degrees Celsius, and the overnight temperature was expected to drop to minus ten. I didn't have a sleeping bag or proper warm clothing, so I decided not to stay at base camp overnight. I'd stay at the monastery guesthouse. I said goodbye to Lynne and the others and hopped into the next available pony cart. I smiled all the way down the mountain.

MY FACE FELL when I saw the accommodation at Rongbuk Monastery. The room had concrete floors and metal bunks. There was no heating, insulation or running water. Unsurprisingly, no one else was staying there. It would scarcely be any warmer than sleeping in a tent, as it was only two hundred metres lower than base camp. I actually felt a bit scared and realised I'd made the wrong choice.

I went straight over to the eatery and ordered a beer and a plate of fried rice. It was warm and cosy, with a stove fire in the middle for heating the big pot belly kettle.

There at another table were Kris and Roland. They saw me too, and waved me over. My heart started thumping as I walked to their table. It was another magnificent stroke of luck.

They were so friendly and funny that I felt at ease straight away. Kris showed me some of his photos of Mount Everest before his camera stopped working. I could make out the details of the rock formations – it was amazing. He told me he was a nature photographer and Roland was a war correspondent who had just finished a stint covering the war in Lebanon.

Wow, wow, wow.

Both men were very good-looking, but it was Kris who I felt a strong connection with. My heart skipped a beat when he sat closer to me after he returned with three bottles of beer. We kept talking as we watched the sun dip behind Everest from out the window. There were a few other hikers in there, plus the Tibetan drivers and the café staff, who I think was one large family with several kids aged up to about ten.

Before I knew it, it was almost nine o'clock. I couldn't believe I'd stayed awake so long after such a massive day. Roland announced he was turning in and heading back to their tent. Kris immediately wished him goodnight, making it clear he was staying with me. After Roland left, I confided to Kris that I was scared of how cold I was going to be in the guesthouse. I was actually worried I could get hypothermia. Kris and Roland had erected their tent outside the monastery, but they had proper sleeping bags and thermal jackets and pants.

'Hmm,' he said. 'Maybe we could stay here? It is much warmer in here from the fire.'

'That's a great idea – let's ask.'

We spoke to the matriarch of the café family. She was sweeping out the back. She shrugged her agreement and added some yak dung to the fire, which we thanked her profusely for. Then she switched off the lights and went into the back room, where I saw the rest of the family already asleep on mats. I was so relieved – and also excited to be spending the night with Kris.

'I haven't got a sleeping bag,' I blurted out.

'I do,' he said with a smile. 'I'll go and get it.'

'Okay.'

Kris ducked off to the tent he and Roland were sharing and returned with his sleeping bag. He unzipped it and covered us both as we lay there, looking at the moon, the stars and Mount Everest.

We began swapping life stories, starting from our childhood. Kris said his parents were adventurous, and had been supportive of his ambitions to become a photographer. He listened sympathetically as I told him of the impasse I was at with my plans, and how I felt pressured to go to London.

Kris revealed that his full name was actually 'Krishna'. His parents had spent months in India together before they were married, and they loved it so much they named their only son after a Hindu god. I told Kris how excited I was about going to India.

'I'm also going there!' he said. 'Right after I climb Mount Annapurna in Nepal. It's lower than Mount Everest, obviously, but apparently it's a more challenging mountain to scale.'

'How amazing,' I said.

'You're amazing,' he replied.

Kris ruffled my hair, and then we kissed.

As long as I live, there will be no night more romantic than this.

'Jess. Pssst, Jess. Wake up,' said Krishna while gently shaking me. 'Some hikers are here and they need more seats,' he said quietly.

Blushing, I hopped out of Krishna's sleeping bag. I could see the barely concealed surprise of the hikers that had walked in for breakfast. I smoothed my hair as Krishna rolled the bag before going to order us coffee and food.

We ate fried eggs and toast and kept talking as though we'd known each other for years. Krishna was really funny. He was telling me about a time one of his shoots went hopelessly wrong when Roland burst into the café.

'Good morning, you two lovebirds. Krishna, we gotta leave in ten minutes. The driver wants to go.'

'What – why?' said Krishna, almost angrily.

'Because he has to pick some people up in Old Tingri. We will lose our ride if we don't go now,' said Roland. 'The driver came to tell me to tell you.'

There were no public transport options between Everest and Kathmandu, so Kris and Roland were hitchhiking there. They'd arranged the first lift with a driver who was returning a jeep to a travel company.

'Well, it looks like I have to go now,' said Krishna. 'I'm sorry to say goodbye to you.'

'Me too.'

Kris gave me his email address and a beautiful big hug. I smelled his hair as he held me close for a few seconds. And then he walked out the door and was gone.

I waited for the others to come back down from base camp. Part of me was dying to tell Lynne and Louise that I'd hooked up with Kris, but something stopped me. I worried they'd think that was slutty of me.

I hopped into the backseat of the jeep and we began the two-day journey to Kathmandu. My mood was plummeting like the altitude. I kept wondering why the universe set me up to meet a person with whom I had such a strong connection, only to make it so very fleeting. It wasn't fair. I also wondered whether Kris would email me. He seemed to really like me, but maybe it was just in the heat of the moment.

I stared forlornly out the window for hours. Schlomi even asked if I was feeling unwell. I knew I was being melodramatic: I'd known Kris for less than ten hours. But I also knew I hadn't felt such an intense attraction to someone since Matthew.

It didn't help that with the excitement of Everest behind us, the atmosphere inside the jeep was downright snarky. Louise and Lynne bickered in the front seat, Paul scarcely spoke and looked strained all the time, the driver *never* spoke and Schlomi permeated sadness. She cut a lonely figure as she stirred her pot of kosher stew on the stove that night. If the trip had helped to restore some of her self-confidence, it wasn't evident on the surface.

I began to brighten as we finally grew closer to the Nepalese border. Clumps of wildflowers appeared in the barren, stony landscape and the air had a balminess to it that made my heart sing. Champa drove cautiously along a steep path with a ravine and a river below, and at one point had to stop while a herd of yaks passed us from the other direction. Their shaggy black coats looked so warm and soft, yet they were also immensely powerful creatures, with long curved horns and muscular shoulders.

We farewelled Champa at Rasuwagadhi Fort on the border and walked into the immigration building. I sailed through customs, revelling in the ease of communicating with officials who spoke English. They smiled at me with such warmth. Louise and Lynne had their knickers in a knot behind me. I was pretty sure a breakup was on the cards for them back in London.

The five of us got into a banged-up minivan Lynne had booked and we set off for the six-hour journey to Kathmandu. After passing through stunning scenery of rice paddies and shacks, the traffic got progressively worse. We spent three hours at a standstill on a clogged highway. It was warming up and I was desperate to change out of my trousers and long-sleeved top, and I got a cramp in my leg from the confines of the backseat. Then Louise and Lynne had the worst fight I'd seen them have over the past week. It was about which hotel they were going to stay at. All I knew was that I would make sure that I wasn't staying in the same one.

I ignored the tension in the air and tried to focus on looking out the window. I was going to love Nepal. I already loved the mishmash of colourful shopfronts and tiny alleyways. I saw a monkey sitting on top of a little shrine on a street corner, and a couple of dogs were rummaging through a pile of garbage. The tourists looked like hippies. The street food smelled amazing.

We got stuck behind a semi-trailer full of oranges and lemons, then I was agog when I saw an enormous bull on the road. It must have weighed five hundred kilograms. How could it be so calm in the midst of chaos? Why was it not charging? The bull moseyed over to the gutter to start snacking on some cabbages. I saw a blond-haired guy taking photos of it. He looked just like Kris. I blinked. It was Kris!

Without thinking, I yelled out, 'Stop! Stop! I'm getting out.'

I grabbed my backpack and leaped over the back seat as though I was escaping a burning building. If I took too long, Kris might disappear into the crowd without knowing I'd seen him.

'Open the door!' I shrieked. I leaped from the vehicle. 'Bye!' I called out as an afterthought.

I ran over to Kris and tapped him on the shoulder. He spun around. He looked at me, and I saw him do a double take. Then he broke into a huge smile.

'Jess! What are you doing here?'

'I've just come from the border crossing. We were driving past when I saw you taking photos. The jeep is over there,' I said.

But the jeep was already out of sight.

'I can't believe it,' said Kris, still looking kind of stunned. 'What an amazing coincidence. And what incredibly good luck.'

'Maybe it was meant to be.'

THANKS FOR READING

Would you like to read the forthcoming sequel to Once Around the Sun?

Kathmandu to the Khyber Pass will be published in 2025. It covers the seven months Jessica spent in Nepal, India and Pakistan. Follow Jessica Mudditt on Instagram, Facebook, LinkedIn or Amazon for release details.

Are you writing a nonfiction book?

Jessica Mudditt is the founder of Hembury Books, which provides coaching, editing and self-publishing support. Set up a discovery call with Jessica through her website - hemburybooks.com.au or email jess@hemburybooks.com

www.ingramcontent.com/pod-product-compliance
Lightning Source LLC
LaVergne TN
LVHW031604060526
838200LV00055B/4479